STRIKE IX

Paul Lonardo

Copyright © 2009 by Paul Lonardo

All rights reserved. No part of this book shall be reproduced or transmitted in any form or by any means, electronic, mechanical, magnetic, photographic including photocopying, recording or by any information storage and retrieval system, without prior written permission of the publisher. No patent liability is assumed with respect to the use of the information contained herein. Although every precaution has been taken in the preparation of this book, the publisher and author assume no responsibility for errors or omissions. Neither is any liability assumed for damages resulting from the use of the information contained herein.

ISBN 0-7414-5690-7

Published by:

INFINITY
PUBLISHING.COM

1094 New DeHaven Street, Suite 100
West Conshohocken, PA 19428-2713
Info@buybooksontheweb.com
www.buybooksontheweb.com
Toll-free (877) BUY BOOK
Local Phone (610) 941-9999
Fax (610) 941-9959

Printed in the United States of America

Published November 2009

PREFACE

In May, 1991, Brown University was dealing with a recurring budget dilemma and a current shortfall of $1.6 million. Unless drastic measures were taken, the deficit would continue to grow out of control. The Ivy League institution needed to do what many other private sector companies around the country had already been doing during this period of economic recession: downsize.

Brown President, Vartan Gregorian, took immediate action by announcing a moratorium on new hiring and directing all departments throughout the university to cut their budgets to stave off the deficit. The athletic department, doing its part, withdrew funding from four varsity teams; men's golf, men's water polo, women's gymnastics and women's volleyball. These teams were allowed to continue to compete at the intercollegiate varsity level and remained eligible for post-season tournament play, but they had to raise their own funds. When the women's gymnastics and volleyball teams encountered funding difficulties that threatened the futures of their sports, they decided to seek a remedy through the legal system, something Amy Cohen, a junior gymnast, knew a little something about as the daughter of a judge.

In April 1992, a class action lawsuit was filed against the school by nine female athletes, led by Cohen. In what became known as *Cohen vs. Brown University*, the plaintiffs sued the university claiming that by cutting support for women's teams, the school was not in compliance with the NCAA's gender equity and proportionality strictures, or more specifically, Title IX of the Educational Amendments Act of 1972. This federal law, enacted by the U.S. Department of Education and administered by the Office of Civil Rights (OCR), prohibits sex discrimination in educational institutions. It states that, "No person in the United States shall on the basis of sex, be denied the benefits of, or be subjected to discrimination under any education program or activity receiving Federal financial assistance."

Although the most prominent "public face" of Title IX is its impact on high school and collegiate athletics, the original statute made no direct reference to athletics. What the legislation does cover are *all* educational activities, whether it involves academic opportunities themselves or other aspects of academic life.

What is quite clear about Title IX is that it applies to an entire school or institution if any part of it receives federal funds. Thus, athletic programs are bound by this rule even if there might be very little direct federal funding for the school's sports programs specifically.

In the lawsuit, the women athletes at Brown alleged that at the time of the cuts their male counterparts had already enjoyed the benefits of a disproportionately large share of both the university resources allocated to athletics and the intercollegiate participation opportunities afforded to student athletes. Thus, plaintiffs contended, what appeared to be the evenhanded demotions of two men's and two women's teams, in fact, perpetuated Brown's discriminatory treatment of women in the administration of its intercollegiate athletics program. The women were represented by Trial Lawyers for Public Justice (TLPJ), an advocacy group in Washington, D.C.

Since the advent of Title IX, schools have been increasingly threatened with discrimination lawsuits, but that same year, 1992, the U.S. Supreme Court held (in *Franklin v. Gwinnett County Public Schools*) that schools which failed to comply with Title IX could be sued for compensatory and punitive damages.

In its own defense, Brown University asserted that it was a national leader in women's athletics, ranking second in the number of NCAA-sponsored sports it offered females. Moreover, the institution pointed out that nationally 69% of those who participated in intercollegiate athletics were male. That, Brown claimed, was a ratio that their university far exceeded. The school maintained that the cuts they made affected sixty athletes in roughly the same male-to-female ratio (60-40) as was representative of the entirety of its varsity athletes at that time. Brown further claimed that to accommodate the request of *Cohen* would require the university to either find additional funding to continue expanding women's teams or eliminate opportunities for men, which in and of itself, they argued, would conflict with Title IX, resulting in the men's programs suffering at the expense of the women's programs.

Brown, basically, refused to buckle under the pressure of the lawsuit. A line had been drawn in the sand, and with the two sides at odds the battle had begun. Only this battle would not take place on the field, but in the courtroom.

Immediately, TLPJ attorneys asked for a preliminary injunction that would require Brown to reinstate funding for the two women's teams and to refrain from any further cuts in women's sports until the case could be heard on its merits. After some legal wrangling, the preliminary injunction was granted in April 2003 and Brown was forced to restore funding for the teams during the 1993-94 season. That fall, the *Cohen vs. Brown University* trial got underway and lasted more than three months. The following March, after review of all the evidence and testimony, U.S. District Court Judge Raymond S. Pettine entered his final opinion. He found Brown in violation of Title IX and ordered the school to reinstate the women's programs, giving them 120 days to submit a proposed plan to come into full compliance.

The ruling came after it was determined that 897 students participated in intercollegiate athletics at Brown University in 1993-94. Of that number, 62% (555) were men and 38% (342) were women. During the same period, Brown's undergraduate enrollment comprised 5,722 students, of which 49% (2,796) were men and 51% (2,926) were women. Brown's intercollegiate athletics program consisted of 32 teams, 16 men's teams and 16 women's teams. In 1993-94, then, Brown's varsity program afforded over two hundred more positions for men than for women. Accordingly, the court found that Brown maintained a 13% disparity between female participation in intercollegiate athletics and female student enrollment and stated, "Although the number of varsity sports offered to men and women are equal, the selection of sports offered to each gender generates far more individual positions for male athletes than for female athletes."

What this ruling suggested was that "participation opportunities" at an institution are defined solely by a hard gender count of it student athletes.

Judge Pettine stayed his order pending appeal, and Brown announced that it would, indeed, appeal the ruling to the First Circuit Court of Appeals. On Brown's behalf, three organizations, representing more than 1,700 American colleges and universities, filed briefs of *amicus curiae*. This Latin term literally means "friend of the court," and is someone (or group) who is not a party to the litigation, but who believes that the court's decision may affect its interest.

In July 1995, while the appeal was pending, Brown presented its compliance plan to the court. Hoping to keep all of its men's sports intact, they suggested placing participation caps on them while also requiring that its existing female teams recruit more players. They proposed creating junior-varsity squads in five existing women's sports and requiring existing teams to meet minimum squad sizes. Judge Pettine promptly rejected the university's compliance plan, ordering them to provide full funding for three donor-funded women's varsity teams and to advance one intercollegiate club team to fully-funded varsity status.

In spring 1996, the U.S. Court of Appeals for the First Circuit in Boston heard arguments from both sides and later that year a three-judge panel reached a decision. They affirmed in part, and reversed and remanded in part the decision reached the year before by Judge Pettine. The First Circuit reversed a remedy ordered by the lower court that would have required Brown to provide full funding for the women's teams that were specifically mentioned. The 2-1 decision concluded that the school had the right to determine which teams receive University-funded status, as long as the plan comports with the requirements of the law.

Despite the partial victory, Brown steadfastly denied that they were out of compliance with Title IX and appealed the case to the U.S. Supreme Court, a move supported by more than sixty other colleges and universities. However, in April, 1997, the highest court in the country refused to hear the case, so Brown proposed a new compliance plan, to which the lawyers for the plaintiffs objected, sending the case back into the Rhode Island courts. However, before the scheduled start of the trial the following summer, Judge Ernest Torres approved the preliminary settlement, effectively eliminating the need for the hearing. A formal notice of the settlement was distributed to the class members at the start of the 1998 fall semester.

Under the terms of the agreement in *Cohen vs. Brown University,* Brown was required to guarantee funding for women's gymnastics, fencing, skiing and water polo. The university would also have to ensure that the women's intercollegiate athletic participation rate remains within 3.5 percentage points of the female undergraduate enrollment rate at the school. And if Brown eliminates or downgrades a current women's team, or adds or upgrades a men's team without adding or upgrading a corresponding women's team, then the school must ensure that women's intercollegiate athletic participation rate is within 2.25 percentage points of women's undergraduate enrollment rate at the school.

PART I. THE TEAM

It breaks your heart. It is designed to break your heart. The game begins in spring, when everything else begins again, and it blossoms in the summer, filling the afternoons and evenings, and then as soon as the chill rains come, it stops and leaves you to face the fall alone.

- A. Bartlett Giamatti,
former Major League Baseball Commissioner

CHAPTER 1   ROSTER MOVES

A BREED APART

Even before the Providence College campus officially opened in the fall of 1998, there were at least thirty of the nearly 4,000 incoming and returning students who could not wait for the semester to begin. What distinguished these young men from any others was something they already had in common, and something else that they would experience together that year. Their shared excitement was not for the academic excellence that the school provided. It was not even the prospect of all the pretty girls from around the country that PC attracted every semester. All of these things, and more, would be part of their total educational experience at Providence, but these boys were there for just one thing. Big East baseball was on their minds.

Besides their gloves, spikes, bats and other gear, they packed their suitcases with so many hoodies and sweatpants that there was little room for anything else. They left their homes and families that summer, confident in their abilities and expecting success on the field. And why not? Many of them were the best at their positions in the high schools and towns where they played before being recruited to Providence. They had practically been romanced by the Friar baseball program that had become a perennial powerhouse in the Big East during the decade of the 1990's. The team was coming off a 31-22-1 record in 1998, and though they fell short in the Big East Tournament, Head Coach Charlie Hickey saw great promise for 1999. The nucleus of the team was returning, and there were several outstanding recruits that had been added.

BATTERY POWER

Going into the season, Providence's pitching staff might have been the team's biggest question mark. While senior starters Marc

DesRoches, Josh Burnham and Rob Corraro could be relied on, the rest of the arms were questionable.

Marc DesRoches, the 6-2, 220 lb. right-hander from Cambridge, MA, was the undisputed ace of the staff. He was a graduate student of psychology in his final year of eligibility, and was a team co-captain. Marc was an exemplary role model for the younger pitchers, with a work ethic that was second to none. He would take his turn in the rotation no matter how much he might have been hurting, and if he didn't have his good stuff on a particular day he would find a way to win. He started experiencing elbow trouble during the 1998 season, but he still led the Friar staff with eight wins.

Rob Corraro, the big 6-7 righty pitcher from Madison, CT was projected to be the number two starter. He was a hard thrower who had a great deal of confidence and was not afraid to challenge hitters. He came into his own in 1998, making the most out of his starts and really learning how to pitch. In high school, Rob excelled at basketball as well as baseball. He had been named a *USA Today* basketball All-American and was chosen in the 15th round of the 1995 Major League Baseball draft by the Toronto Blue Jays. He was offered a signing bonus of $100, 000, but decided to go to college instead to complete his education and hone his pitching skills.

Josh Burnham was slotted as the number three starter. The senior right-hander from Tolland, CT was listed as 5-11, but his teammates knew that was a stretch. He was not a big guy, but he could throw hard and pitched with a lot of heart. Always tough and durable, he stepped into the Friar rotation in 1998 as a junior college transfer student and won six games. He could consistently throw strikes while moving the ball around the plate. He kept hitters off balance by changing speeds and mixing his pitches, which included a sharp breaking ball. Josh was a fierce competitor on the mound who knew what it took to win.

While these three were expected to eat up a lot of innings at the top of the rotation, this year's Friar team also had a wealth of untested arms. A baseball team can never have enough pitching, but Coach Hickey didn't know what he would be getting in 1999. One thing he was counting on was that the competition would make the pitchers, and the team, that much better.

Todd Murray, a senior right-hander from Andover, MA, was regarded as one of the hardest throwers in the Big East. He used his very good changeup as an effective set-up pitch. He had primarily been a set up man in 1998, but his stuff was dominant enough to close. He had recovered fully from elbow surgery his sophomore year, which caused him to miss the entire 1997 season.

Scott Swanjord was a 6-5 senior right-hander and elder statesman on the team at 23-years old. He was a hard-thrower who didn't begin his collegiate baseball career until he was a junior. He spent his freshmen and sophomore years as a goalie on the Friar hockey team. The Fairfax, VA native attended high school in Anchorage, Alaska and was picked by the New Jersey Devils in 10th round of 1994 draft. He had been a very good pitcher in high school, as well as a skilled goalie, and had spent a couple of years playing hockey in a Midwestern league before enrolling at PC. However, his ice time at Providence was limited, so in 1998 Swanny decided to try out for the baseball team. Even though it had been more than four years since he had pitched, he was athletic and confident in his baseball skills. To everyone's surprise but his, Swanny made the team as a walk-on, getting his feet wet with a few innings that season. He was anticipated to be the long relief man in 1999, and could play some spot outfield.

Andy "Stork" Scott was a crafty left-hander from Milltown, NJ. He was only a sophomore, but he already had excellent control and command of his pitches. He made the most out of his opportunities during his freshman campaign. He exhibited intelligence on the mound and an ability to work hitters, setting them up by moving the ball around. He kept everything low and induced a lot of groundballs, an ability that would play in his favor because of the slick fielding defense behind him, especially up the middle. He was a tough competitor who was not afraid to go after hitters, and was anticipated to be the lefty out of the bullpen when the 1999 season began and a spot starter.

Sophomore south paw, Mike Stuart, had seen a lot of action as a starter and a reliever in 1998. He showed a lot of composure and an ability to pitch in pressure situations. He made four appearances in the 1998 Big East Tournament, including one start. Stewy was expected to be the top left-handed relief pitcher for the Friars.

Josh Cox was a solid right-hander who sat out the 1998 season with an arm injury. The senior from Cambridge, worked as both a starter and a reliever during his career at Providence College. He threw hard and he threw strikes, with excellent command of all his pitches. He would be given an opportunity to throw in middle and long relief for the Friars in 1999.

Brett Donovan was another sophomore lefty. He hailed from Riverdale, NY and was especially tough on lefties, making him a potential to be the left-handed specialist out of the bullpen.

Brendan Ryan and Ryan Lewis rounded out the crop of incoming freshman hurlers.

Ryan Lewis was a lefty from Newport Beach, CA. He became the first Friar from the Golden State. He had impressive stuff for someone his age. Although he was not overpowering, he had all the tools to excel in the college ranks. He knew how to work hitters, had excellent mechanics and got great movement on his ball. More importantly, he threw strikes.

Brendan Ryan, a Canton, MA native, was an outstanding athlete, who played multiple sports in high school and excelled at all of them. He could play the outfield as well as pitch, and could be called on to pinch hit, as well.

George Colli was a returning sophomore pitcher, but that summer a routine check-up led to the discovery of a pre-cancerous testicular lump which required immediate surgery. It turned out to be a benign tumor, but because of some minor post-operative complications he needed the entire fall, maybe longer, to recover and get back into playing shape.

Sophomore backstop Dan Conway from Delmar, NY would be doing the catching for Friars. As a freshman in 1998, he backed up Scott Friedholm, a third team ABCA All-American. Dan was being asked to fill some pretty big shoes in 1999, but his coaches as well as the pitching staff had a lot of confidence in him. Conway was loaded with potential, possessing all the catching tools, including a powerful throwing arm. He was a quiet team leader who did so many things to help the team win which do not show up in the box scores.

AROUND THE HORN

To compliment the experience and depth of the Friar rotation was an offense that set numerous records in 1998, a season in which they hit 80 homeruns and combined for a team batting average of .335. Returning sluggers Keith Reed, Angelo

Ciminiello and Mike O'Keefe gave the Friars one of most potent 3-4-5 hitters in the Big East.

Keith Reed, the junior outfielder from Auburn, MA was an imposing figure with a bat in hand. His tremendous bat speed generated a lot of power. His teammates called him "Reggie" because of his flair for hitting the ball a long way when he got behind one. He slugged 14 homers and drove in 58 runs in 52 games in 1998. He was an outstanding athlete who had worked hard and improved his entire game exponentially in the two years he'd been at PC. He could do it all, a five-tool player with nothing short of a cannon for a right arm. Keith was the type of player who could dominate a game in the field or at the plate.

Angelo Ciminiello, senior third baseman from St. James, NY was a quintessential scholar-athlete. As the team's other co-captain, he was a leader both on the field and off. He was a hardworking, intense player, who earned everything he got, including a First Team All New England selection in 1998. Considered a contact hitter who used the entire field, Angelo also had plenty of power. With twelve homeruns in 1998 to go along with a .376 BA, he was someone the team came to rely on in clutch situations. And talk about versatile, Angelo pitched in short relief in 1998 and that same year moved from left field to third base, quickly showing that he was more than capable at the hot corner. His teammates described him as a silent lion, a good guy who was always polite and respectful to everyone, but he was intense, as ferocious as anyone when he got fired up. Opposing pitchers found that out often, and occasionally his teammates did as well when they did not display the respect for the game or the discipline that it took to play their best.

In the classroom, Angelo shined equally as bright. He was a Big East Academic All-Star in 1998 and had been named to the GTE/CoSIDA District I Academic All-America team.

Sophomore first baseman Mike O'Keefe was coming off a stellar freshman season with the Friars, hitting .332 with eight bombs and contributing with his glove as well. He was a Big East All-Rookie selection in 1998. The Hamden, CT native was an outstanding fielder and a powerful offensive threat from the left side of the plate. As a high school senior, he was selected in the 18th round of the Major League Baseball draft by the Anaheim Angels. Okie was a prototypical cleanup hitter, who could do a lot more. He was considered a total package ballplayer by the coaching staff, and arguably one of the most talented players on the Friar squad.

Middle defense, taking away hits and turning double plays, has always been a key to successful Friars teams of the past. Milton, MA senior, Paul Costello, was considered one of the top second basemen in the Big East. A solid fielder, with only 7 errors and a sparkling .972 fielding percentage in 1998, Paul was a steadying influence in the middle of the diamond. He was also one of the team's most consistent all-around players. Paul was also an outstanding basketball player in high school, nominated to the McDonald's All-American team in 1994.

Joining Paul up the middle was incoming freshman, Jamie Athas, a left-handed hitting shortstop from Holyoke, MA who possessed all the athleticism and tools to be an outstanding Division I shortstop. He had excellent range and a strong arm. At the plate, he was a line-drive hitter who was always on base and was a threat to steal, possessing both speed and quickness. There may not have been a more athletic Friar on the squad, playing baseball and basketball three years in high school, football and soccer two years.

Great things were also expected of another incoming freshman, Neal McCarthy, who joined the Friars after attending Florida Southern for a semester. From Warwick, RI, the homegrown product had four years of eligibility remaining. He had an outstanding high school career, a three-time All-Stater from Bishop Hendricken High School, the same parochial school attended by Major Leaguer, Rocco Baldelli. The left-handed swinging outfielder/DH was a hit waiting to happen anytime he has a bat in his hands.

Mike "Scooter" Scott was academically a sophomore, but because he sat out his freshman year due to a knee injury, he had four years of baseball to look forward to at PC. The leftfielder from Darien, CT was a solid all-around player, a line drive hitter with speed. He could play centerfield if called upon to do so. He was a hard worker and not afraid to get dirty, and as good as he was no one could have predicted the kind of year he would have for the Friars.

Junior outfielder, Jason Hairston, was a speedy defender who could cover a lot of ground. At the plate, the Rockville, Maryland native was a contact hitter who could turn infield ground balls into hits. Breaking into the starting lineup in 1998, he hit to a tune of

.339. On the base paths, he made things happen, and was one of the few guys on the team who had a green light. He had stolen 19 bases in 21 attempts that year. He was also one of the best bunters on the team, dropping down a team-high eight sacrifices.

Junior Jeremy Sweet was perhaps the most versatile Friar. Like many Friars, he played and excelled in multiple sports in high school, and that athleticism was reflected on the playing field that year. He served primarily as the Friar's right-handed designated hitter, but he also played first base, third base and could catch. He had a potent bat and developed ability to hit in the clutch.

Another junior who saw more playing time in 1998 was Coley O'Donnell. The prominent 6-3 220-pounder from Sudbury, MA served as the Friar's left-handed DH and occasional first baseman. He had excellent power, and even though he had a tendency to strike out, he was a threat off the bench as a pinch hitter who would be called upon to ignite late inning rallies for the Friars. He hit 6 homeruns in only 85 at-bats the previous season.

Freshman Matt Ciardelli from Milford, NH was a solid young backup infielder. He had good speed that could be exploited in pinch running situations. Versatile, he could play short or third. He also had strong hitting credentials with an ability to get the bat on the ball and some occasional pop.

Brendan Trainor, a freshman from Chelmsford, MA, was another addition to the 1998 squad who was expected to contribute. He could provide solid depth to the Friar infield, playing second and third base. He made good contact at the plate and hit line drives.

CHAPTER 2   FALL GUYS

RITES OF PASSAGE

As fall practice got underway, the returning players became re-acquainted while the newcomers got to know their teammates. The guys, for all their similarities on the field in skill level, drive and respect for the game, off the field they were very different. The mixing of so many unique individuals inevitably produced some volatility. Most of the guys got along well enough, but there were some personality clashes. There was plenty of ego and pride to go around, as well. With so many talented players, there was no shortage of confidence.

A healthy dose of trash-talking was tolerated as the players prepared themselves for the long season ahead. Cliques formed, along with the natural separation between the "veteran" players and the "rookies." The rooks needed to know their place. It was part of baseball, no matter what the level of play. This indoctrination process was sometimes a painful one, as freshman Jamie Athas found out one fall afternoon.

Like the other freshman coming in who were the best players on their high school teams, Jamie's world was suddenly turned upside down when he became a Friar. There was actually a good mix of youth and experience on the 1999 team, with several exceptional underclassmen, of which Jamie was one. However, he was still a freshman, just another kid trying to earn some playing time. He had to prove himself all over again. This rite of passage was something Jamie learned about quickly when he tried to joke around with one of the seniors, just as he would have done to any of his other teammates. The senior was co-captain, Angelo Ciminiello, who gave Jamie the first real lesson of his young college career.

Jamie had been joking around with the starting third baseman because he had been getting some innings on the mound during their intrasquad games. Every time Jamie saw him on the hill he

Strike IX

would say things out loud like, "I can't wait to hit off him," and "Look at those balloons coming in. Is it somebody's birthday?" He made sure Angelo heard him, but the team captain never said anything back so Jamie didn't think much of it. Then one afternoon Jamie got his chance to bat against Angelo, and it was an experience he would not soon forget.

Angelo's first pitch sailed behind Jamie's back, striking the chain link fence with a clank. Jamie was still green enough to be unsure if it was an accident or if Angelo had thrown at him on purpose. The confusion was quickly cleared up when Angelo uncorked his second pitch, another fastball which drilled the freshman on the ass. It left a welt that lasted for days and an even longer-lasting impression with regard to whom he could joke around with and who he could not. After practice, he approached Angelo and offered an apology, which was accepted. Lesson over.

Another newcomer who got off on the wrong foot with an upperclassman was Ryan Lewis, a typical, carefree and quirky California kid, some might even say a little weird. That was a judgment call, but what wasn't opinion was that his eyesight was bad. Ryan wore contacts and could not see at night or in the dark. While he was pitching, he had a habit of manually adjusting the disposable lenses in his eyes so he could see better. It was during an intrasquad game one morning that everyone on the team, and in particular Jeremy Sweet, found out just how bad Ryan's vision really was. Jeremy was doing the catching, and when he put down two fingers signaling for a curveball Ryan could not see the sign clearly and guessed fastball. He guessed wrong. When Ryan threw the pitch, Jeremy started to move his glove across the plate to where he expected the ball to break, but it never did and he didn't have time to adjust to the velocity. The baseball struck Jeremy square in the groin and he instantly dropped to his knees, doubled over in agony. Of course, everyone on the field started laughing. Everyone except Ryan, that is. Jeremy was in a lot of pain and it quickly became apparent that he was not going to be able to just walk this one off. As his teammates gathered around the fallen catcher, Ryan just wanted to hide. Jeremy had to be helped off the field. He was almost taken to the hospital, as his testicles had immediately swelled up like grapefruits. Lots of ice was used to reduce the inflammation and the next day Ryan compensated Jeremy for the cross-up with a thirty-pack and all was forgiven.

Very quickly, the guys started to gel, though not all of it happened on the field.

ODD COUPLES

A lot of the players shared living space together, with many of the upperclassmen staying in off-campus housing and the freshmen and sophomores in school dormitories. Some of the living arrangements paired the most unlikely of teammates.

Keith Reed showed up at PC the son of a Pentecostal Minister. He didn't smoke, drink or stay out late. Then he roomed with Jeremy Sweet, who was as boisterous as anyone on the field. He chatted constantly and enthusiastically from the dugout, almost to the point of *ad nauseam*. In street clothes, Jeremy was much the same, with an affinity for rap music that he and Keith shared. Some would say he was a bad influence on Keith, others might say that he brought his roommate out of his shell and spared him from the sheltered life he lived up to that point. The truth may be somewhere in between, but Keith was no fool. He knew that if he kept his focus on baseball, he could punch his own ticket to the Majors. He was twenty years old, away from home, and he didn't see anything wrong with having a little fun along the way. At parties at night, Keith was known to break out into song, rapping about the team, mentioning each player. Jeremy would usually accompany him, beat-boxing beside him, providing the rhythmic harmony for Keith's ditties. But this was just practice. Sometime during the 1998 season, the duo took their hip hop routine to the field, performing their rap when the team would gather in a circle before the start of each game. It soon became a tradition. A team anthem, of sorts. Some of the other players would join in, providing additional background harmony or "popping" in time to the beat. Mike O'Keefe and Josh Burnham may have enjoyed this pregame ritual most, as they were pretty heavy into the rap music scene themselves.

Seniors Paul Costello had lived with Todd Murray the previous couple of years. While Paul met his future wife when he was a freshman and dated her throughout his four years at PC, Todd went in the complete opposite direction when it came to women and dating, which was many and often. In fact, Todd might be best remembered for what he accomplished in the

Baseball House rather than on the baseball field. If he saw only limited action on the field that year, off the field it was another story. There is usually a ladies' man on every team, and if there was one on this Friar baseball team, it was Todd. There were always a lot of pretty girls around the Baseball House, which Todd turned into his own private brothel. In one instance for which Todd is famously remembered, he was in an upstairs bedroom with one girl while two other girls were waiting for him downstairs, like patients at a doctor's appointment.

One thing Dr. Love never seemed to have, according to Paul, was food. He never went to the market, and instead had a habit of staring at Paul like a starving dog when he saw him eating. At first, Paul would give in and ask Todd if he wanted some of what he was eating. Todd never refused. Finally Paul got wise to this and began to ignore his roommate, hoping that when it was no longer offered to him he would go out and shop himself. Paul wasn't sure how successful this approach had been. He never saw a grocery bag, but Todd managed to maintain his stamina somehow as the girls kept coming around.

Andy Scott had been labeled "Stork" by his teammates because he was tall and gangly. The name was given to him the year before by senior pitcher Doug "The Buzzard" Wall. Everyone thought they looked a lot alike, so the moniker "Stork" was born, and it stuck. Very quickly, no one called him by his first or last name, not even Coach Hickey. He was simply the Stork. During that fall semester before the 1999 season, Stork was staying in the same dorm, on the same floor but opposite ends as Mike "Scooter" Scott, who lived with Mike Stuart and a third roommate, a golfer. The sophomores all got along well. Scooter didn't drink, but on nights when he got tired of studying, to unwind he would take a putter from his roommate's golf bag and go out into the hall with two plastic cups. Sometimes he would wake up Stork, and the two of them would take turns putting across the long hallway, reading the breaks in the carpeting. They would do that for hours some nights.

The previous year, Stork lived in the same dormitory with Dan Conway. Dan was on the third floor and Stork was on the first, and just about every night they would meet down in the student lounge to play ping pong. They were pretty good and the games were competitive. Most nights, Angelo would walk by the dorm on the way to his apartment after a late night of studying at the library.

Some nights he would see his teammates inside and knock on the window to be let in. He would play for ten minutes, maybe twenty or so, and he would beat the pants off both of them and then just leave.

Stork was amazed by this at first, but then after seeing Angelo play the infield, it was easy to see why he was so good at ping pong. Angelo had about quickest hands he had ever seen. While Stork was behind second base collecting the balls during infield practice, he would marvel at the skill Angelo displayed with his glove.

During rain delays or in the locker room after practice, Angelo would showcase another talent he had with an empty chewing tobacco tin. While Stork and some of the other guys would grab a bat and take turns swinging, Angelo would proceed to put on a clinic with the dip can. He could throw those things like a Whiffle Ball, making them move in all directions, sinkers and risers. It was incredible. Nobody could hit his dip.

THE BASEBALL HOUSE

Each semester, a number of the older players, predominantly seniors, resided at The Baseball House, an old two-story home on Tyndall Street, just outside campus. But you didn't have to be a senior, or a baseball player, to visit The Baseball House. It was a place for the players to relax, drink and take girls.

The house also happened to be the boyhood home of Brian Feeny, who owned the nearby bar, Bradley Cafe, a favorite neighborhood watering hole of Providence College athletes and scholars alike, and certainly not an unfamiliar location to the coaches and players of the Friars baseball team. More times than not, after a night of socializing at Brad's, the party would continue at The Baseball House with a keg for what came to be known as, "Late Night at Tyndall." For the players who spent time there in 1999, at least, the two-family tenement was more than just an Animal House for jocks. Although anyone else who dropped by would be hard-pressed to see it as anything other than what their five senses told them: the place was an absolute sty. Second floor residents Chris Caprio, Paul Costello and Marc DesRoches, as well as Mike O'Keefe, Josh Burnham, Joe Rigabar, the team's student assistant, who occupied the first floor, didn't seem to mind. And while the neighbors may not have been keen on the foul smell and overall squalor of The Baseball House, there were some members of the local community who were more than comfortable there.

As the story goes, the players who lived at the house the previous year realized that they were sharing their quarters with an uninvited houseguest. This discovery was made late one night after a party when Paul Costello, asleep on an upstairs couch, was awakened by the sound of something rummaging around the apartment. In the darkness, he saw something crawl under the couch he had been sleeping on. Paul immediately jumped to his feet, making enough noise to wake the rest of the house up. He was startled by what he thought was a squirrel. The rodents were abundant in the trees all over the neighborhood. When everyone came down stairs, however, and they turned the couch over they discovered a rat the size of a small dog.

As soon as the critter was revealed, you might never see some of those guys move any faster on the field than they did at that moment in their underwear. They scattered. Some jumped up on tables and chairs. In the confusion, the rat got away and no one saw where it went, but it was never far away. For the rest of the semester, the players shared the house with the rat, which became familiar enough that they began to call it "Ricky". Although an altogether arbitrary name, identifying the rodent as such suggested that it was taking on pet status. Ricky would be heard from time to time, usually at night as he rummaged around the house for leftovers, but no one saw him again until one fateful night when Ricky met an unceremonious demise and was exterminated by two seniors and a nine iron.

PASTIMES

Baseball may be America's nationally recognized pastime, but for students on college and university campuses across the country, casual sex and binge drinking remained the unrivaled recreation of choice. Providence College was hardly exceptional in that regard, if the behavior of the baseball players were any indication, anyway. Without getting into graphic detail, there were always a bevy of Friarettes around the Baseball House. However, this is not an indictment on the PC women, nor is it meant in any way to suggest that the female Friars were easy, far from it – the exploits of Todd Murray notwithstanding. For the rest of the team, when it came to success with the girls at The Baseball House, it was like the game itself; you win some, you lose some. For some of the players, they won a lot more than they lost. For others, they just couldn't seem to score no matter what they did.

One of the most retold stories that fall involved freshman Brendan Trainor and a pretty senior co-ed, Kiley Garraghan. She had been working as an assistant for Coach Hickey the last couple seasons, helping with the scheduling and other tasks. Because of her duties, she was around the team a lot and everyone knew her. Almost everyone, that is. One night at bar, Brendan started to hit on her. Kiley knew who he was but decided to play along and engage him, asking him questions about himself. When Brendan, hoping to improve his chances with Kiley, told her that he was a senior on the baseball team, she could no longer contain her laughter and told the freshman that she was his coach's office assistant. Brendan did not find it as funny as the rest of his teammates when they heard that he tried to put the moves on Kiley.

For the Friars with proper ID, and the cash for a door cover and $10 beers, they could visit the Foxy Lady just down the road for some adult entertainment. Stories abound about local athletes and the popular Providence strip club, but those involving Friar ballplayers, including the one with two senior pitchers and their encounter with reigning porn queen of the time, Ms. Jenna Jameson, you won't hear about here.

When it came to beer and related drinking games, PC could compete with any school, Catholic or otherwise. Sneaking booze into underclassmen dorms and tapping kegs at The Baseball House were as commonplace as the crucifixes on the walls of the classrooms or the standing room-only crowds at the 10:30 Sunday night masses. There was a lot of beer pong going on at Brad's between the baseball players and members of the men's lacrosse team that season. It was another way in which the players were able to bond and relieve some stress at the same time.

Not all the players participated in these kinds of extracurricular activities, however. Senior starting pitcher, Rob Corraro, like Scooter, was not much for drinking. For all his intensity on the mound and his love of rap music, Rob was a quiet and sensitive guy. On a team full of Type A personalities, some of them A-plus, he practically flew under the radar. Even his closest teammates didn't know much about him. Rob was somewhat mysterious. He was a transfer and had a girlfriend who did not attend PC, but that was about all most of his teammates knew about him. However, whether it is on the field, in the dorm or at the bar, you can learn a lot about your teammates. Some of those things you don't necessarily need to know. Other things you may not want to know.

With Rob, there was at least one mystery that his teammates figured would never be solved. On the back of his spikes, above the heel, were the initials "TMBA," and Rob never talked about what the letters stood for. No one wanted to ask him either, because it was assumed the initials represented something that was very personal, and if Rob didn't feel comfortable bringing it up on his own, then it would not be appropriate for anyone to ask him. The prevailing belief was that they were the initials of close friends of Rob's who had died, perhaps killed in a car accident. But then one day during the 1998 season, curiosity got the best of fellow pitcher Doug Wall, who pointedly posed the question, "Rob, what the hell does TMBA stand for, anyway?"

Without hesitation, Rob proceeded to tell Doug that his favorite movie, as well as his girlfriend's favorite movie, was the Tom Cruise 80's classic, *Top Gun,* and that they both loved the song from the film; Take My Breath Away. TMBA was the initials in the song's title.

It took everyone's breath away when that was revealed. Rob's disclosure immediately brought to Doug's mind a couple other initials: TMI.

CHAPTER 3   THE LAST TO KNOW

THE RUMOR MILL

Rumors had begun circulating that Providence College was going to cut some of it men's sports programs even before the ruling had been made on Brown University's Title IX sex discrimination lawsuit. Some PC athletes had heard the whispers, but the administration never confirmed or denied the allegations, so the discussion remained merely background noise. That fall, however, the static started to pick up its intensity.

Baseball was certainly not excluded from the debate, but no one really believed that America's pastime would be one of the programs that a catholic school, so steeped in tradition, would simply eliminate to improve their bottom line. With the success that the baseball program had enjoyed in recent years, the threat just wasn't taken seriously. Swimming or track, or any one of the other sports, really, would be the program or programs that everyone thought would be the first to go.

While the game clock on several Providence College sports was ticking down to zero, the individual male athletes whose programs were targeted for elimination were completely unsuspecting. Conversely, school administrators had known for quite some time which teams were in their last days. The announcement was forthcoming, and the secret needed to be kept just a little longer. However, as the semester got underway, the students who were around the administrative offices began to notice an inordinate number of men in suits coming and going. One of those students was Dave Regan, who worked in the office of the Vice President for Student Affairs. It was not difficult for him to determine that these men were attorneys, and for whatever reason he was under the impression that some kind of lawsuit involving the women's hockey team was brewing. That got the student thinking about contacting a friend who worked for the college paper, *The Cowl*. He thought his friend would be interested in pursuing the story further. The friend he contacted was Joe Valenzano who, besides being a sports writer for the school paper was also the statistician for the baseball team. Joe was very interested. When he began to look in the story, the first person he talked to was Brian Tamul, a former PC baseball player and graduate student who worked as an assistant in the Athletic Compliance Office.

Brian sounded a bit anxious to Joe as soon as he brought up the subject of the lawyers on campus. Brian refused to speak over the phone, and arranged a meeting in the rafter seats of Alumni Hall where they could talk in private. Joe thought it was very odd, and did not understand the need for all the secrecy. However, once they started talking Brian told him off the record that baseball was on the chopping block and that it was probably going to be one of several men's varsity teams eliminated by the college at the end of the academic year.

Joe was stunned, even more so because this story was totally different from the one his friend had given him. There was no way this was not going to make the next edition of the paper, he thought to himself. Even though Brian refused to be named as the source, Joe ran the information by the paper's Sports Editor, Ken Martin, who was also a one-time member of the Friar baseball team and had played alongside Brian. Another clandestine meeting was arranged, this one between Ken and Brian, who was fearful of losing his grad assistantship for speaking out. The two met in the back of a car one night in a parking lot off campus, and Ken reassured his former teammate that under no circumstance would his name be disclosed. Brian trusted him and revealed everything he knew.

TRUTH AND CONSEQUENCES

When Ken returned from the meeting with Brian, he told Joe that they were going to write the story, listing Brian as an unidentified source. The two school journalists put in some very late hours trying to get the piece completed before that week's deadline. It was close, but they got it in just before the copy went to print. There was no time to even have the story approved by the college administration, which looked over the content of everything that went into *The Cowl*. Truth be told, there was a very real concern that the administration would not approve the story, so a more conscious effort was made to sneak it by them. In going forward, they knew they were taking a great professional risk. Then, on Thursday, October 1, 1998, the headline in the sports section of *The Cowl* read, "Title IX Enters Eleventh Hour."

The article addressed the gender equity disparity at Providence College head on, reporting that several men's teams were in jeopardy as a result. Citing an unspecified source within the Athletic Department, it was speculated that baseball might very well be the sport that would be eliminated by the college in order to comply with NCAA regulations regarding Title IX.

In print now, in black and white for everyone to read, the shadowy rumors were suddenly transformed into something more substantial. The article generated an instant buzz around campus and among the PC athletes. It also rattled the cages of college administrators, who threatened to shut down the entire newspaper if the source was not revealed. Ken and Joe were the only ones on the paper's staff who knew it was Brian, and they were not about to give him up. They called the school's bluff and won. Shutting down the paper then would have only underscored the conclusion drawn by the article and affirm what had been written. Besides, the administration had more important issues at hand.

To the utter amazement of those responsible for the story, word quickly spread far and wide about Providence's Title IX problem and the phones began ringing off the hook all around campus with calls from sports columnists representing regional and national newspapers. Ken and Joe knew they were on to something big, but they didn't know just how big until an editor from *Sports Illustrated* contacted the college to verify the story.

The administration did not immediately respond, but they knew they had to do something, and fast. A plan was quickly devised over the weekend to answer the claim. It was determined that before they made any public statements they should first sit down with the coaches and athletes of the sports programs that were going to be impacted by the cuts, and that it should take place as early the following week as possible. They would need Monday to finalize all the details, so the college set Tuesday, October 6, as the day of reckoning.

A BOLT FROM THE BLUE

When the players got onto the field that afternoon, it was a picture perfect fall day, with mild temperatures and plenty of blue sky and sunshine. They had just started working out when Coach Hickey was suddenly called away to attend a meeting, and that changed the entire complexion of the practice. It was more than just not having Coach around to run the team through their drills and bark Hick-isms at them when they messed up. The other coaches and team captains could handle those things well enough, but the players all sensed that something was wrong. From the unannounced meeting to the persistent rumors to *The Cowl* article, it was all too much to overlook.

It was like an oppressive wet blanket had been tossed over them, dampening their spirits. They spent the next hour or so playing long toss, or pepper, just trying to stay loose. Before too long, that activity degraded until they were all just milling around. They were busting balls and joking as usual, but even their light-hearted banter had an air of uneasiness to it. They could have officially ended practice and gone back to their dorms, apartments, girlfriends, barstools, but they didn't. They didn't know when Coach Hickey might get back, but none of them were going anywhere until he returned.

After gathering up the equipment and raking the infield, Coach Hickey finally walked back onto the field, about an hour and a half after he had left. He walked slowly across the infield, just inside the third base line, shadowed by his coaches. He motioned for the players to gather around near home plate. He looked like someone had punched him in the gut.

"This is bad," he began.

None of the players seemed to be breathing.

"The college is cutting the baseball program," he said quickly, like pulling a Band-Aid off.

He looked around at the shock and disbelief painted on the faces of his players.

"It's official," their coach informed them. "1999 is going to be last season for baseball at PC."

Marc DesRoches, the big right-handed ace of the staff, had to take a knee. He had been through so much with the program. After his freshman year he had considered moving on from PC. That year, 1995, the Friars were ranked 15th in country, and he appeared in only 1.3 innings. Discouraged, he sat out the entire 1996 season, and returned the following year only to throw a total of 9.3 innings. Marc bounced back with a solid 1998 campaign. Despite pitching through pain that limited his success, he still won eight games.

With his eyes clouded, Coach Hickey tried to focus on the one positive aspect that remained by telling the team that they would still have the season to play out and that all they could do was win as many games as they could to put pressure on the administration into rethinking their decision. He had no other answers for his players. There were still many questions that Coach Hickey had himself for college administrators, as well as a few choice words, but he didn't share any of that with them. Instead, he informed them that the Assistant Athletic Director wanted to meet that evening to talk to them about Title IX and why the baseball program was being eliminated.

Additionally, Coach Hickey advised his team to take the rest of the week off from practice and to use the time through the weekend to talk with their families and think about what they wanted to do with regard to their futures at Providence College.

By 7 p.m. a brief closed door meeting between the players and the administration took place in the college press room. Assistant Athletic Director, Mark Devine, addressed the athletes. He explained the reason for the school's decision to cut baseball, along with golf and tennis, the two other men's sports programs that were being eliminated in order to comply with Title IX mandates. After he spoke, he allowed the players to ask questions, but most were too angry or upset to respond. They were all still in a state of shock after getting the news from their coach. Some cried, some got angry and some kept their emotions to themselves, but for all of them it was a moment in their lives that they would never forget.

DECSION 1998

Title IX was something that not every member of the Providence College baseball team had been familiar with prior to this stunning announcement. Many knew about it to varying degrees, but a few had not been aware of the federal law at all, including freshman, Jamie Athas. After the article came out in *The

Cowl, Athas went back to his dorm and *Googled* "Title IX" to find out more about it. Even senior, Paul Costello, had to admit that he had no real knowledge of Title IX. In the coming months, both Paul and Jamie, along with their teammates, would learn all there was to know about this anti-discrimination act. For all of the Providence College baseball players in the fall of 1998, however, it could be said that until that otherwise perfect October afternoon, the significance of Title IX seemed altogether foreign, a distant concern, at least, like a skirmish in some remote part of the world between two countries whose names they could not even pronounce. It was something that had little or no impact on their small world of Big East college baseball. But that had suddenly all changed.

For Mike Scott, it was more like what Yogi Berra would have referred to as '*déjà vous* all over again.' It was the second time that a college baseball program had been pulled out from under his feet. While still in high school, and captain of the basketball and baseball teams, he had all but signed a letter of intent to go to the University of New Hampshire to play baseball, but then he learned that they were dropping the program because of a Title IX problem. When Scooter decided on Providence College, he thought that an issue like that would be the last thing he had to worry about. He could not believe that it had happened to him again.

Junior outfielder, Jason Hairston, was also devastated by the news. Like others on the squad, he had chosen PC specifically because of its baseball program. As a high school senior in Connecticut, Jason made All-State in soccer and baseball and he had been heavily recruited in both sports by such institutions as the Naval Academy, West Point, and Boston College. Some considered him a better soccer player, but he chose to pursue his options in baseball because of his love for the game.

The atmosphere and location of Providence College, as well as the reputation of its baseball program in the prestigious Big East Conference, not to mention the academic opportunities, inclined Jason to choose Providence.

The qualities that enticed Jason to Providence were the same ones which had recently been helping the school attract the top ballplayers from all around the region and produce the best baseball teams in Providence College's history.

The unexpected demise of Providence's baseball program forced Jason to make a tough decision. He had already completed two full years of studies, and if he played his junior year at Providence, the team's last season, it was unlikely that he'd be able to transfer to another school and play in his final year of eligibility. And even if he had transferred successfully to another school to play his senior year, it would cost him academically. Most schools do not accept three years of academic work, so transferring would delay his graduation for at least a full year.

When Jason originally signed his letter of intent with Providence College, he planned to play four years of Division I baseball with the goal of getting drafted, which was not an unqualified pipe dream. In the 1990's, PC had produced several players who went on to play Major League Baseball, including Lou Merloni and John McDonald. Providence had also been consistently producing prospects that were sprinkled throughout the minor league system year after year since the mid 1980's. Now, if Jason chose to stay and play out the 1999 season as a Friar, he would have to give up on a dream, but it was a decision he did not have to think long about and it was one he would never regret.

There were other student-athletes with difficult choices to make. Juniors Jeremy Sweet and Coley O'Donnell were in the very same boat as Jason. They were juniors, but if they decided to stay at PC their college baseball careers would end that season. All of them, however, had made up their minds to graduate from Providence, remaining through 2000 without a team to play for.

Not all the players accepted their fate so easily. To the man, they experienced the full range of emotions associated with the grieving process. Initial disbelief and sadness quickly gave way to anger. They felt abandoned, betrayed and disrespected by a college administration that did not seem willing to fight to save their program. It was difficult not to take it personally. An uncontrollable fire had been lit inside every one of them. It was them against the world from that moment on, and the funny thing was they all seemed to like it that way, even thrive on it. Holding onto that anger would become a tremendous motivating factor, and they were determined to take that anger out on any team they played and use it to accomplish something special that year.

CHAPTER 4   AFTERMATH

PICKING UP THE PIECES

Coach Hickey *had* heard all the rumors before and he understood that compliance with Title IX was a serious matter. The landmark court case that had recently been decided on the other side of the city, at Brown University, was still fresh in everyone's mind. The lengthy and expensive legal process had ended with the court ruling in favor of the female athletes, and that fact was not lost on Father Smith or the other Providence College administrators. The coach was also well aware that twelve other Division I schools had cut their baseball programs in recent years, opting to avoid costly litigation and take preemptive measures to comply with the law, so PC was hardly alone in such a dubious distinction, or rather *extinction*. There had been rumblings as far back as eighteen months that the school needed to address their own gender-equity problem. Coach Hickey, however, was still shocked by the finality of the decision and upset that it had been kept from him, making him look foolish in front of his team. He was angry that he did not have any say in the matter. It was the feeling of complete powerlessness and utter irrelevance, which he resented more anything else.

At first, he did not know how his players would react. *How many of them would even bother sticking around*, he wondered. The biggest challenge he faced that season might be just keeping the team together and fielding nine guys who could compete in the Big East Conference. Among the phone calls of outrage and sympathy that Coach Hickey received from the other schools in the hours immediately after the announcement was made public were inquiries about the availability of his players. His fellow coaches came swooping in like vultures to take what was left of the team that he had assembled, the talent that he scouted and cultivated. This upset him, but in a way he couldn't blame them.

After all, they weren't the ones who had put him and his players in this situation.

A CALL TO ARMS

Immediately following the meeting with the Assistant Athletic Director, the players decided to organize an assembly of their own, to come together as a team, and to host a party for the ages at the Baseball House, to get fucked up, loud and laid. In that sense, the party was of the typical variety for the Baseball House and the team in general; there was a whole lot of testosterone and Solo cups being flipped. And there were plenty of hot chicks. There were also numerous alcohol-inspired proclamations made by players about how "this sucks" and "we need to show them." Several upperclassmen, including Angelo Ciminiello, Paul Costello and Keith Reed, gave more impassioned speeches. Paul, in particular, went all out to get everyone's attention. At one point he jumped up on a table, yelling, kicking beer bottles and cups around the room. He wanted to be sure everybody was fired up and ready to fight back. His call for unity was taken to heart, as almost immediately a slogan was born, or rather reborn, which was adopted as the official rally cry for the 1999 Friars baseball team. It would later be printed on T-shirts which all the players would wear under their uniform jerseys the entire season.

"THERE'S ONLY ONE THING LEFT TO DO..." was emboldened in white letters on the front of the black shirt. On the back; "WIN THE WHOLE %@!()& THING."

It really did say, %@!()&. This is a Catholic school, after all, but the sentiment was unmistakable. They were fucking pissed. The phrase was a motivational gimmick taken straight out of the 1989 hit movie, *Major League*, about a pro baseball team that had to overcome great odds and win a championship or be dismantled. Providence saw themselves as just such a team. They were on the brink of elimination, but they were determined not to go quietly. They would be unified in an effort to practice hard that fall and then go all out the entire season and win, not only to prove to the school administration but to prove to themselves that they were winners.

The players unanimously agreed not to take any time off, and to practice right through the weekend.

The "pep rally" ended with a boisterous chant of "Omaha...Omaha...Omaha!" in reference to the site of the College World Series and the player's individual commitment of helping the team reach the tournament in June.

PARTY NAKED

The night was far from over, and from there, things got really rowdy, as might be expected when emotions and alcohol mix. Along the way, some windows got busted, a few couches and rugs were stained with booze and vomit and some beds were pissed on. But it was all good.

The party shifted to Bradley Café, before the night ended with a group of players driving a keg down the street to Hendricken Field. They sat on the dirt and sod of the diamond under a starry night sky, draining beer from the tap and telling stories about some of the things they had seen and did on the field. They probably would have stayed there reminiscing until the sun came up, but then a couple of the guys took off their clothes and started streaking around the bases. The screaming and laughter drew the attention of the campus police, who were extra vigilant that night. They were anticipating the possibility of vandalism by angry students in the wake of the program cuts. As soon as the players saw the high beams and the spotlight trawling the darkness around them, they left the keg behind and scattered. They scrambled over the fences, some partially clothed, and dispersed in all directions through the streets of the surrounding neighborhood until they made it back to their dorms and apartments unscathed.

NO MAN LEFT BEHIND

Ultimately, only four players – three freshmen and a sophomore – transferred due to the demise of Providence's baseball program, determining that it would be in their best interest to pursue their academic and athletic goals at another school in 1999. The other players, as well as coaches, did not hold their decision against them. Everyone understood. Coach Hickey promised to do everything he could for any of his players to help get them into another program at another school. He vowed to do the same for the players who still had eligibility left at the end of the 1999 season.

One of those freshmen who left was catcher, Jon Nathans, who went on to play ball at the University of Richmond before signing as an undrafted free agent by the Boston Red Sox in 2001. Nathans might be best known for the August 14, 2007 incident in which he was injured while catching for the independent Bridgeport Bluefish. Former Major Leaguer, Jose Offerman, was batting as a member of the Long Island Ducks when he was hit by a pitch and charged the mound with his bat. Offerman swung twice, striking the pitcher's hand with one blow and Nathans' head with the other. Nathans suffered a serious concussion and lingering effects from the assault. He later sued Offerman and his team, seeking millions in damages, as Offerman was charged criminally and received probation.

For the PC players who remained, seniors and underclassman alike, the decision to stay hinged on one thing, collectively playing as hard as they can to have the most successful team in school history and show the administration that they were making a huge mistake cutting their sport. In the back of their minds, some of them were thinking that if they went on to win the Big East or perhaps even the NCCA Division I title, they might be able to save baseball at PC. However, if that did not happen, they knew they still had something to play for, and it was the one thing that nobody could take away from them; their pride.

CAMPUS REACTION

The next day, Father Smith met with the parents of some of the players. There were a lot of emotions, and for all the talking that the college president did, he provided few answers, which only heightened the frustration level of everyone. It was a big mess.

The players were just happy to get back out onto the field. Even though it was a drizzly, rainy day, there was nowhere they would rather have been. There is just something about throwing a baseball around that seems to block out all of your troubles. It's a truly magical thing. Despite the depressing atmosphere in the dugout and in the skies above, as they divided up for an intrasquad game, they all played hard, busting their asses on every play. The added purpose of playing to prove their worth lit a fire under them that would burn undiminished the entire season. It was a fire from within, but it was sparked by a school administration that had let them down, dismissed them and the game that meant so much to them. They were not playing for PC history, not even for the future of the program. They were playing for each other now, nothing more.

The same day, Alumni Gymnasium became the site of a protest by for more than two hundred PC athletes, male and female alike, who had not been affected by the cuts. They gathered to voice their displeasure with the college's proposal to eliminate three men's teams in order to comply with gender equity requirements. John Marinatto, the Providence College Athletic Director, was there to listen to them.

Many of the student-athletes expressed a feeling of betrayal for the displaced members of the men's golf, tennis and baseball teams who were not given any forewarning that their programs were ever in jeopardy. The other major concern was what those athletes were going to do the following year. Marinatto tried to defend the college's decision, vowing that they would do everything they could to help the displaced athletes transfer to other schools, but that courtesy only underscored how the school seemed all too willing to cast them aside in the first place.

Joe Valenzano expressed the same feeling of betrayal by the school administration in an article he wrote the following week for *The Cowl*. He sharply criticized the school hierarchy for throwing around the words *tradition*, *pride* and *commitment*, but not knowing their meaning.

Elsewhere around the school, everyone did what they could to support the banished sport. From making personal appeals to the school to reconsider the cut to raising public awareness with campaigns that included fundraising and organized protests, the student body as a whole rallied around the team. Bumper stickers that read SAVE PC BASEBALL were distributed around the state. And it wasn't just the students who made their objections known. Some faculty members were unafraid to express how they felt. One popular history professor wore all black as a tribute to the baseball team for a better part of the semester.

What may have been most surprising to some was how Providence's female athletes vociferously decried the cuts. Those who spoke up publically all agreed that something else could have been done in order to achieve compliance. In a show of unity for their male counterparts, the women's field hockey, soccer and tennis teams threatened to not play their upcoming games. In the end, however, they did not want to add further disgrace to the damaged reputation of the college's sports programs and wisely reconsidered their boycott. They played their scheduled games, though the volleyball team, hosting Brown University, of all teams, expressed their solidarity by wearing PC baseball uniform jerseys while they were warming up before their game.

PC Swimmer Michelle Hackmer told The New York Times, "When the announcement was made about eliminating baseball, the women athletes were as mad about it as anyone else." She added, "Sure we want women athletes to be treated fairly, but at this expense? I don't think this is what Title IX was supposed to be about."

She effectively made the point that was shared by many people, recognizing that the problem was with the bureaucratic regulations and enforcement policies, not the statute itself. However, the reality remained that without remedial policy changes, men's teams at college and universities around the country would continue to be sacrificed at the Title IX alter. Unfortunately, such changes do not come easily, and it was already too late for PC baseball.

PROS AND CONS

The men's golf and tennis programs at Providence were effectively given a stay of execution when they were permitted to raise money privately to keep the teams functioning, if only temporarily. The baseball program, however, was not granted such a reprieve. Raising money to save the baseball program would not even be considered. This was something that incensed many, including alumnus Lou Merloni, who at that time was an active member of the Boston Red Sox. He had been selected a co-Big East Player Of The Year as a senior at PC before being selected in the 10th-round pick of the 1993 draft by the Sox. When he learned about his alma mater's plight, he made an immediate beeline from his home in Framingham, MA to the Providence College campus. He, too, wanted answers. Real Answers. He met with Father Smith behind closed doors and discussed the matter for a half hour before speaking with A.D. John Marinatto as well as Coach Hickey.

Father Smith, a 1963 PC graduate who was elected the 11th President of Providence College in 1994, told Merloni that the decision was out of his hands, a buck he quickly passed to the Board of Trustees. Merloni, along with many others, were hoping to be afforded an opportunity to help bail out the baseball program by raising private funds to cover team expenses indefinitely, until the another solution to the Title IX compliance issue was devised. After proposing this suggestion as one possible measure that could be taken to save the sport, the Major League second baseman was informed by Father Smith that this was not a viable solution and that there was nothing that could be done. Merloni was bemused and frustrated by the lack of explanation.

The need to satisfy Title IX requirements was easy enough to understand. Cutting men's programs could even be justified. What Merloni wanted to know was *why baseball*? The sport was the oldest at Providence College and the program was enjoying its most successful years at that time. Providence had earned berths into the NCAA regionals two times in the previous seven years, winning the Big East Tournament title in 1992 and the regular season conference title in 1995. He left with no real answer to that question.

Before heading back home, Merloni stopped by the locker room after practice just to see how the team was doing and to let them know that he supported them, which meant a great deal to the players. Everyone who was there that day got a lot out of hearing this Major League ballplayer speak about the importance of staying focused and achieving a common goal.

AROUND THE NEIGHBORHOOD

The decision to eliminate baseball as a sport from Providence had a strong impact on the neighborhood and people who lived in the vicinity of the campus. One local who felt the loss of the baseball program on a personal level was "Plumber."

Just about any maintenance or mechanical problem involving the PC athletic department, Plumber was the guy who took care of it, though he didn't work for the college in any official capacity. He was a jack-of-all-trades as well as a master plumber, and he enjoyed helping out the sports programs in any way he could. He didn't do it for the college. He did it for the student-athletes. Even though Plumber was close to the baseball players, few of them knew him by his real name. He was just Plumber to them. If you asked any of them who Pat McCarthy was, they wouldn't have a clue.

Baseball might be a summer sport, but in college and universities around New England the game is played in the worst possible climate for much of the year. The seasons are short and the field conditions are far from ideal. Friar ballplayers are outside playing games in the calendar months of winter. It takes a lot to get a field ready in this area of the country, and Plumber was there to do whatever was needed to ensure that baseball could be played on any given day.

Plumber would plow snow off the field in February, heat the pitcher's mound when the dirt would frost-freeze in March and pump water off the infield after spring rain flooded it.

Through the years, Plumber put in untold hours getting the various athletic facilities at Providence College prepared so games could go on as scheduled. He would often use his own money to purchase various items that were needed to complete a job. For their part, the administration had always silently resented Plumber's contributions, tolerating it because he was essentially providing free handyman services. Right from the start of the 1999 season, however, beginning in the fall of 1998, that started to change dramatically. Once the program was on the chopping block, Plumber's services were no longer appreciated by the college administration. It was something that would become more and more apparent as the season progressed.

Plumber, as well as the coaching staff and the players, realized they were on their own that year. And if that was the way it had to be, then that was fine. They would do it all themselves.

Brian Feeny, owner of the popular Bradley Cafe, had lived in the shadow of Providence College his entire life. Through the years, he and Plumber would often stop by Hendricken Field to catch a few innings of most games. They would meet in the same spot behind the backstop fence, where several other regulars set up their lawn chairs to take in a ballgame. Many of those in attendance knew one another; neighbors, students, friends and family members of the players. There was occasionally some real homegrown talent that came through the school's baseball program, guys like Paul Rizzo from North Providence. He was someone you rooted for as a Friar and later followed his progress in the minors because not only was he a talented player, but he played the game the way it was meant to be played.

Providence had always drawn strong interest from the best ballplayers around New England, but more recently the talent pool had expanded to include all regions of the country. Recruitment had become top notch by 1998. Year after year, Friar teams were loaded with skilled, dedicated players. It was good, quality baseball. And it was all free, which was something that almost certainly made the sport dispensable in the eyes of the administration.

For guys like Plumber and Feeny though, it was more than just a way to kill an hour or two a couple afternoons each week during the spring. This year, the players and the fans would be sharing something truly special, which they would appreciate like no other season before.

CHAPTER 5   TITLE IX

ONCE BITTEN

Providence College administrators certainly had been keeping close tabs on how *Cohen vs. Brown University* played out. Their Ivy League neighbor spent seven years and $7 million fighting a Title IX compliance complaint in the courts. Providence College clearly did not have the financial resources to mount that kind of defense, nor did they believe that they possessed as strong a record of support for women's athletic programs as Brown, who even with all their advantages still lost their case. The Catholic College simply did not think that they had a prayer if similar litigation had been filed against them, and they gave up without a fight.

By 1998, Providence College would have already conducted their own litmus test and realized that they had a failing grade. Title IX regulations require all institutions receiving federal funds to perform self-evaluations to determine whether they are in compliance. The principle enforcement activity conducted by the Office of Civil Rights (OCR) is the investigation and resolution of sex discrimination complaints. OCR has the discretion to randomly select an institution for review in order to assess its compliance with Title IX, even in the absence of a complaint. In the event of violation, OCR possesses the authority to affect voluntary compliance and negotiate appropriate remedies.

From the introduction of the 1972 legislation there has always been some question as to the best way to determine compliance to the mandates of Title IX. Then, in 1979, the U.S. Department of Health, Education and Welfare issued a final policy interpretation regarding Title IX and intercollegiate athletics by introducing a three-pronged test for assessing compliance.

> Prong one – Providing athletic opportunities that are substantially proportionate to the student enrollment.
>
> Prong two – Demonstrate a continual expansion of athletic opportunities for the underrepresented sex.

Prong three – Full and effective accommodation of the interest and ability of underrepresented sex.

A recipient of federal funds can demonstrate compliance with Title IX by meeting any one of the three prongs, though most academic institutions opt to comply with the first prong, known as the "proportionality prong."

In 1999 at Providence, the student body population was comprised of approximately 59% females and 41% males. However, 54% of the athletes were males, who also received the majority of athletic scholarships.

The NCAA insists on 1% gender-equity proportionality, meaning that the percentage of female students and the money spent on their sports must be within 1% of the men's athletic budget. Using the proportionality prong to comply with Title IX, Providence College needed to have at least 58% of the school's total athletic funding appropriated for women's programs. In conjunction with this, a 58% share of all athletic scholarships would have to be earmarked for female athletes.

Looking strictly at these numbers, Providence was way out of compliance, even though at that time participation by women in collegiate sports continued to trail enrollment rates of women at colleges and universities around the country, according to The Chronicle of Higher Education. Nationally, women constituted 53% of all undergraduates on Division I campuses, but only 40% of the participating athletes. By this barometer, the numbers at Providence College were typical, but that was not the measure the OCR or the NCAA were using as their gauge. Title IX was the Golden Rule.

ADDITION BY SUBTRACTION

Since its inception, the "three-prong test" has been highly controversial in its interpretation and enforcement, and there is disagreement over how best to analyze its effectiveness in achieving its intended purpose, which is to eliminate discrimination on the basis of sex in federally-funded educational institutions. Critics of the three-prong test argue that it operates as a "quota" in that it places undue emphasis on the "proportionality prong" and fails to take into account the differing levels of interest with regard to the gender of athletes. Some go so far as to say that this interpretation of Title IX goes beyond its original purpose and violates the statutory language of the Fourteenth Amendment, taking athletic opportunities away from male students and actually discriminating against men.

Defenders of the three-prong test, however, claim that the sexes' differing athletic interest levels is merely a product of past discrimination, and further contend that the three-prong test embodies the maxim that "opportunity drives interest."

One result of the "quota" standard that can hardly be argued is that it has forced many schools to eliminate or spend less money on minor, non money-making men's sports programs such as wrestling, cross country and volleyball. The translation is that it has become more difficult for men to get into large, Division I schools to play "small" sports due to the added emphasis on revenue-generating sports, such as football.

Subsequent studies have shown that while male participation in sports had risen approximately 5% between 1981 and 1998, male enrollment during those same years rose almost 19%. As a consequence, the number of men's sports teams available per male student declined 21% over that time. And although there are now more teams available to women than to men, the total numbers of male participants still significantly outnumber women. In 1999, there were 232,000 males participating in college athletics compared to 163,000 females.

More unsettling were the results of the NCAA's first Gender Equity study, conducted in 1992. The five-year follow up, published in 1997, revealed a highly disturbing downward trend for male athletes. During that time period, more than 200 male teams and over 20,000 male athletes had been lost. Over those same five years, the number of female athletes increased by only 5,800. This equates to nearly four male athletes lost for each new female athlete added.

While statistical analysis has shown that ninety-five percent of the gains for female athletes have been seen at the Division I level, what's more interesting, and alarming, is that at the Division III level, where there are no athletic scholarships and student athletes play purely for the love of the game, the effect of Title IX has been simply disastrous. During the same five-year span of the NCAA Gender Equity study, it has been shown that in Division III schools only 178 female athletic opportunities had been added while male opportunities were reduced by more than 9,000. That represents the loss of twenty males for every female gained in Division III collegiate sports.

So what went wrong?

There can be no arguing that females faced a shortage of athletic opportunities through the 1970s. A year before Title IX's passage, only 294,015 girls played high school sports, compared to 3.7 million boys. In the succeeding decades, women's participation in school athletics has increased impressively. During the 1999-2000 school year, at the time of the Providence/Title IX controversy, 2.7 million girls played high school sports, compared to 3.8 million boys, according to the National Federation of State High School Associations. In 1998-99, 148,803 women played NCAA sports, up from 80,040 sixteen years earlier.

Considering the overwhelming statistics, there remains one question above all others that begs an answer: Is there ample reason to suspect that there is more to gender disparity in school sports than lack of opportunity?

Institutions today have, indeed, increased sports opportunities for females, yet males continue to turn out in far greater numbers. Stated simply, women have more chances to play sports today but they do not take advantage of them. Some have offered valid explanations for this.

"Girls are interested in more things," said Kimberly Schuld, a consultant on gender equity issues for the Independent Women's Forum, a conservative, DC-based organization that has been critical of Title IX. "They are more likely than boys to participate in multiple extracurricular activities, not just sports. If we applied a gender quota to other activities, it would destroy opportunities for girls in fields such as journalism, law, and science. Who would stand for that?"

College coaches are not alone in challenging the idea that discrimination is at the root of these numerical disparities. "There's no question in my mind that women are less interested in playing sports than men," said Lamar Daniel, a former investigator at the Department of Education's Office for Civil Rights who conducted the very first Title IX investigation in 1978. Daniel went on to conduct over 20 reviews before retiring in 1995 to become a consultant. "But logically, in my experience, you can't prove that," he adds. "It's just not provable." In practice, Daniel says, this means schools must seek proportionality, either by adding women athletes, cutting or capping men's teams, or doing a little of both.

Clearly, the intent of the regulation is to give more women an opportunity to play intercollegiate sports and to provide it without gender bias or discrimination. Though the law was not intended to reduce the number of men from participating, that is exactly what happened at Providence College in 1999. That is addition by subtraction, and that was where a lot of people around Providence, and elsewhere, had a huge problem. Title IX was not written as a gender-based affirmative action policy for schools to follow, so there had to be another way for PC to comply. College administrators, however, didn't even try to come up with alternative solutions to the elimination of the baseball program.

MONEY BALL

In the gender equity debate, few people blame Title IX itself. Almost without exception, male coaches and athletes say they agree with the spirit behind Title IX. The problem here is in interpretation, particularly by those dictating hard gender-based quotas. Because the actual text of Title IX is relatively brief, when discrimination suits are brought forth the courts have very little to go on. Most of the problems lead back to Prong One and two otherwise innocuous words, *substantially proportionate*, which when joined together no one seems to know how to define.

In theory, compliance with Title IX should not be difficult for any institution to maintain. All they have to do is offer a proportionate number of teams for women and the problem would go away. But it is never that easy, especially when there are other factors for a school to consider, and those factors all involve money. As a consequence, when athletic departments sit down each year to face their growing deficits and shrinking revenues, gender equity becomes more than just a principle, it is a budget item.

Providence College provides a vivid example of the unfortunate way that Title IX often plays out. No attempt was ever made to create new teams for women, and instead the male-female equity gap was reduced by the elimination of three men's sports.

"We didn't want to do this," said Athletic Director, John Marinatto, regarding Providence's decision. "No one embraced this. We didn't have much choice given the financial resources we have. We want to achieve equity and be as competitive as we can in a league that has significantly more resources than Providence College."

The Women's Sports Foundation issued a position paper on Title IX and the elimination of men's varsity sports, stating, "Most schools cite, as the reason for their decision (to eliminate men's athletic programs), the need to reduce expenditures in order to provide opportunities for women. Title IX requires no such reduction in opportunities for men. The Foundation is not in favor of reducing athletic opportunities for men as the preferred method of achieving Title IX compliance."

At direct odds with this statement was Deborah Brake, an attorney with the National Women's Law Center, who expressed her belief that the only problem with Title IX is that it hasn't been enforced comprehensively enough. She told one reporter that she would like "to bring immediate law suits against as many universities as possible to force them to comply with the law." In June 1997 alone, Brake's group had filed 25 complaints with the Office for Civil Rights to celebrate the 25th anniversary of Title IX's passage.

The Office for Civil Rights and the NCAA have forced schools into the unsavory position of needing to meet an illegal gender quota, and athletic directors often take the easiest way out of their gender equity problems by cutting the number of male participants and male dollars.

Defenders of the current Title IX status quo continue to point out that "statistical balance" is only *one* way in which an educational institution may demonstrate compliance, and they claim that no such demand for statistical equivalence is in force. However, most schools are given little choice when faced with compliance issues.

Relying on Prong Three, for example, accommodating *interest and abilities*, is an approach that schools do not even attempt. It is just too difficult to prove, as PC administrators contended.

Adding women's sport programs and offering more scholarship money to increase the number of female athletes to satisfy Prong Two was also quickly dismissed as a viable option by Providence College administrators because of the limited financial resources available. Double-digit increases in tuition and overly optimistic fund-raising projects, they said, were unacceptable budget alternatives, so there was never any chance of adding any sports programs for women. And once that was decided, it was really just a question of what men's sports programs would get cut. Providence baseball was sacrificed as a matter of course because it made the most sense budget-wise. Not only were they looking to avoid a potential lawsuit, but they couldn't afford to wait.

Compliance with Title IX instantly assured Providence that it would pass its NCAA certification review, which was scheduled for completion in the spring of 1999. Equity is one of the areas in which Division I schools are scrutinized by the NCAA, and an institution that is not certified can be banned from the NCAA championships. At Providence, this would mean exclusion from the men's Big East Basketball Tournament, a veritable cash cow for the school that they could not afford to have threatened.

Baseball, in contrast, did not generate a dime for the college. However, it did have seven scholarships to give back, scholarships which could be easily redistributed to PC's female athletes. The baseball budget could, likewise, be shifted to women's programs. In such a scenario, the school loses nothing financially while simultaneously creating more opportunities for its female athletes and leveling the gender-equity playing field incrementally. Eliminating men's golf and tennis, as well, just happened to make the proportionality numbers align perfectly, and with the least amount of fallout.

John Marinatto admitted as much. "Baseball, tennis and golf," the AD told reporters, "were the three sports that, when you combine their resources together, delete them from the male side of the picture, and add those resources to the women's side of the picture, put us in compliance with Title IX's proportionality mandate."

According to Marinatto, the elimination of the three men's programs, plus instituting roster maximums for the remaining eight teams along with minimum requirements for the eleven women's teams, would leave Providence with about 300 intercollegiate athletes, 57 percent female and 43 percent male, which was where the school needed to be.

Providence College President, Father Philip A. Smith, backed up the statements made by his Athletic Director, saying, "I do not feel good about the decision to drop baseball, but in the end we had to have our academic priorities come first. We tried other ways, but nothing else worked. It seemed we'd be taking from Peter to pay Paul, and still falling short. Ultimately, I had to make this unfortunate decision."

School administrators wanted everyone to believe that they had run themselves ragged, exhausting every other possible option to bring the athletic program into compliance with Title IX.

"We all sat down and looked at the reality to comply with Title IX," Marinatto said. "When we explored all the alternatives, we were all pleased with none of the above. It was not a proud day for Providence College."

Rev. Terence J. Keegan, Providence's executive vice president said he was "absolutely sick" over the decision that had to be made. He claimed he was a baseball fan, with his own father having played on the PC baseball team in the 1930's, right alongside Birdie Tebbetts, who was a catcher for the Friars at that time and later went on to play fourteen years in the Major Leagues, including a stint with the Boston Red Sox.

"The only upside to this is that we're in compliance with gender equity," Keegan said. "Everything else is a downside. The ill will that has been created with some of our alumni, the anger of the students involved, all the negative publicity. There has been very little, if anything, that has been good about this."

What was "good" was that compliance didn't impact their bottom line. There were at least 7 million reasons to resolve this the way they did; a lesson Brown University taught them.

"We just couldn't risk that kind of litigation," Rev. Keegan told the New York Times in reference to the high-profile court case. "We felt we were backed into a corner."

Providence's solution was to ax the three men's sports teams which generated the least revenue, plain and simple. Tradition be damned. The success of the program did not matter.

Baseball, the longtime Providence College program, was called out on a Strike IX fastball by school administration.

CHAPTER 6   TRAINING DAYS

FIELD GENERAL

Charlie Hickey was beginning his third season as head coach of the Friars baseball team. The Middletown, Connecticut native and 1987 University of Connecticut graduate became the thirteenth head baseball coach at Providence College prior to the 1997 season. He took over for Paul Kostacopoulos, whom he worked under for the five previous seasons. As the team's pitching coach during that time, he helped develop some of the best young arms in the conference, including the 1995 Big East Pitcher Of The Year, Mike Macone. Friar standout hurlers Todd Incantalupo, Andy Byron and Jim O'Brien, all benefited under Hickey's tutelage.

His coaching style was one that stressed fundamentals. He believed that a team plays like it practices. He had a reputation for being tough, but fair. He was a young man, but he was old school, which for his players meant, among other things, a lot of running. The tire drill station and sprinting all morning until some of the guys puked was part of a football mentality he brought with him from his gridiron days. His thinking was that this kind of training was going to make his players tough mentally as well as physically. He worked his players hard to get the most out of them and they respected him for that.

He sometimes yelled and screamed a lot, almost to the point where some might think he was demeaning his players, but there was a method to his meanness. He knew his job. He needed to do everything he could to get them to play their best as individuals and find a way to win games as a team, not be their best friends. Love him or hate him, the players all seemed to respond to his blue collar approach to the game.

On the flipside, the team had their share of fun with him, as well. Their coach had a unique voice that was relatively easy to impersonate, and most of the players did at every chance.

Although Coach Hickey is from Connecticut, he speaks with a quasi-drawl, though it really isn't quite a southern accent. The impressions were always exaggerated and, of course, acted out behind his back, but the players found this activity to be a safe way to defy their coach who was so prone to call them out whenever they did something wrong. One thing that some of the players liked to do after a few beers was to bring up the appearance that their coach and his family made on the television game show *The Family Feud* in the 1980's. Somehow, a tape of the episode had been found and a copy had been viewed by several of the players, who from time to time would stage a mock *Feud*. Someone would act as the host and the others would play the part of the Hickey family. Even those who had not seen the tape would participate, and everyone wanted to play their coach. They would make up funny answers to made-up survey questions and sometimes it became a drinking game. It was usually good for a laugh or two, and a good buzz.

RANK AND FILE

To help him prepare the 1999 Friars for the season ahead, Hickey surrounded himself with assistant coaches that believed in the system he had established. John "Navvy" Navilliat, in his sixth season with Providence, served as the team's hitting instructor and outfield coach. Navvy, a Pennsylvania product, had been coaching baseball on all levels for more than 23 years, including at the college level at Brown University and Bryant College in Smithfield, RI. Under his guidance, the 1998 squad had an overall team batting average of .335. Navvy played a major role in developing some of the PC's best hitters, including major leaguer shortstop, John McDonald.

Sean O'Connor, Hickey's 38-year old pitching coach, was in his second season at PC. He began coaching immediately after his own stellar collegiate career as a starting and relief pitcher ended in 1983 at St. Leo's College near Tampa. A Framingham, MA native, O'Connor coached at Framingham State, as well as Assumption and Brown University.

O'Connor was more of a player's coach. All the guys loved him, not just his pitchers. He would often go over to a player to smooth things out and reassure them after they had been chewed out by Coach Hickey. Even if O'Connor sometimes played the "good cop" to Coach Hickey's "bad cop," the goal was the same; to get the max effort from their players. And it worked.

Coach O'Connor also had the notable distinction of chewing more tobacco than anyone on the team by a wide margin. He actually made his own special blend, mixing the tobacco with honey and God knows what else. The dugout would be covered with a sticky concoction of tobacco and sugar after every game. In warm weather, the spit became a gummy mess that would stick to the players' cleats and gave off a cloying aroma that attracted bees.

O'Connor was an interesting character who the PC pitchers took an instant liking to. One of the oddest things he was known to do was carry around some kind of horse liniment. Like his chew, he prepared this stuff at home, so nobody knew exactly what it was beyond being green and stinking like hell. He would use it on pitchers who had sore or tired arms, claiming it helped them heal faster. Whether it did any good or not was debatable, but he used it all the time.

Jonathan Krot was the newcomer to the coaching staff. The 24-year old Dayville, CT native was fresh out of Eastern Connecticut State University. As a starting outfielder, he helped the Warriors to the 1998 Division III national championship.

Athletic trainer John Rock, along with Kiley Garraghan, Office Assistant and Joe Rigabar, Student Assistant, rounded out the baseball team's support staff.

PREPARING FOR BATTLE

Filling in one of the holes made when a handful of underclassmen transferred out of PC was Chris Caprio, a senior backup catcher who played sparingly during his freshman and sophomore years. He had taken his junior year off completely, but returned to serve as a reserve player in 1999. He would be the team's insurance policy behind the plate in case anything happened to starting catcher, Dan Conway, and if Jeremy Sweet wasn't available or playing another position.

Once the 1999 roster was set, everyone understood that this would be the final baseball team in the history of Providence College. There was instant motivation for all twenty-five members. Their collective mindset had been established the day the school told them they were giving up on them, and you did not have to read what was written on their undershirts to understand what was inspiring them. With all the players committed to the season, Coach Hickey did not have to remind them of the fact that each passing day was one closer to the end of PC baseball and most of their own careers. He did not need to inspire them or browbeat them to practice hard and take their workouts seriously in preparation for a long, challenging season, and that at least made part of his job easier.

There was no formula that Coach Hickey knew for dealing with this kind of situation. Efforts to try to save the program would have to coincide with the main objective, which was to win as many games as possible.

This year, in a radical departure from his personal baseball philosophy, he would not be as concerned with playing games to win while at the same time developing his younger players for the future. There was no future for this program, so he told his squad that he was going to put his best players out on the field and go with the hot hand until it cooled off.

TASKMASTER

As Coach Hickey observed what his players could do on the practice field, he began to mold them into championship contenders. He was impressed with the way this group went about their business every day that fall. From routine batting practice and repetitive fielding drills to situational hitting and intrasquad games, there was a determination in them that gave him a sense of pride that he had not felt before in all his years in baseball. He saw them grow and mature beyond their years right before his eyes. The added pressure on the players because it was the last year of the program would have ripped lesser teams apart, but it seemed to galvanize this group as a club. With something to prove, they wanted to go out a winner.

But that did not mean that Coach Hickey let them off easy. Some of them were still teenagers, after all, and he had to stay on them. He worked them hard every afternoon, so at the end of the week it was natural that they would let loose a little. The coach wasn't about to turn a blind eye to this, last season or not. When practice concluded, he wanted to know what his players were up to off the field and he would dole out appropriate punishment if word got back to him that someone had acted up and behaved in any way that he thought was improper. Just like any mental mistake in practice or a game, he held them accountable.

Penalties often involved reporting to the weight room at 6 a.m. to lift for an hour and then outside to run for another hour in whatever weather conditions prevailed. There were multiple players there every day from October to December, a Breakfast Club for the bad boys of the baseball team.

Coach Hickey was not averse to criticizing a player, especially the freshmen and sophomores, with the goal of trying to get them to think more about something they did wrong so as not to repeat it. Showboating or hotdogging was sure to provoke the coach. One afternoon Mike Stuart was working on PFP's (Pitcher's Fielding Practice) and he made a pretty good diving play covering first base right in front on Coach Hickey, who looked at Stewy, totally unimpressed, and said, "Someday you'll make a pretty good men's league softball player."

Coach Hickey's no-nonsense approach to teaching the game might be best exemplified with an incident that took place when he was the Friars' pitching coach a few years prior. Sophomore Doug "Buzzard" Wall had been pitching in relief against Notre Dame, facing Jeff Wagner, a power hitting first baseman. There were runners on second and third with two outs. Normally, with someone on second base a pitcher will look for the second set of signs from his catcher for a pitch to throw, in case the runner is stealing signs. PC had a five-finger signal for a pickoff, with the next sign indicating the base that the pitcher had to throw to. Buzzard had worked a 3-2 count on the All-American when he looked past the five-sign, thinking it was a throwaway to deceive the runner. Then he saw two fingers and thought the catcher was calling for a curveball. Needing a strike and not wanting to risk loading the bases, it seemed like an unusual call. But Buzzard was confident in his hook and went with it. The pitch completely fooled Wagner, whose legs buckled as he took the pitch for a called third strike. It was the best pitch of Buzzard's life, and he walked off the mound feeling really good about himself. His excitement was short-lived, however. When he got to the dugout he saw his pitching coach approaching him and he thought Coach Hickey was going to say something like, "Nice going, kid."

Instead, he heard, "Wall, you're not pitching for a month." Then the coach walked away, leaving the pitcher who had just worked out of a big jam utterly confused. Buzzard looked over at his catcher, Scott Friedholm, who informed him of the five-finger pickoff play he had missed. That was Coach Hickey.

PET PEEVES

On any team, there is always a player, maybe two, who the coach seems to favor, someone who could do no wrong. Conversely, there is usually someone who gets picked on relentlessly. If Coach Hickey picked on Paul Costello a little bit, then in comparison he picked on Coley O'Donnell a lot, but never Angelo Ciminiello or Mike O'Keefe. Okie seemed to become an instant pet of the coach, who pulled some strings to allow Okie to live in the Baseball House that year. Coley and Okie were both big boys. Whereas Okie was fanatical about his workout regiment, spending a lot of time sculpting his physique in the weight room and eating healthy, Coley carried a little extra weight and was a happy-go-lucky kid that everybody loved.

For the way he played the game, Angelo had earned the respect of everyone, including his coach. The competition for Coach Hickey's approval may have contributed to the somewhat abrasive personal relationship Angelo had with his younger teammate. Angelo and Okie liked and respected each other well enough, but they always seemed to enjoy getting on one another's nerves whenever possible.

Perhaps the one player who was most put upon by Coach Hickey was Dan Conway. Everyone saw the raw talent the sophomore catcher possessed, but perhaps none more than his coach. He clearly had the potential to play beyond the college ranks, and Coach Hickey would push him hard. The entire fall, anytime you would hear the coach raise his voice, which was often, the odds were that it was Dan Conway he was laying into. And you would know it right away, because he would never call him Dan or Danny or Conway, it was always, "Danny Conway..."

One afternoon the team had just spent forty-five minutes practicing relay drills, where the catcher has to call out which base the ball needs to be thrown to from the outfield. The entire time Coach Hickey was screaming at Dan, who never said anything back. He took it all, and he did become a better catcher. You could see it. But after a while, this treatment began to grate on Dan, and he would become frustrated. Still, he never said a word.

During a rundown another time, instead of throwing the ball to third Dan tried to chase the runner down and tag him out before he got back to the bag, but he failed.

"Danny Conway," Coach Hickey said. "Let's do an experiment." He walked over to home plate and took the mitt and ball from Dan. "Alright, take off to third." Dan immediately started running to third and the coach threw the ball to the fielder covering the bag. After Dan was tagged out easily, Coach Hickey yelled, "Now, stop. Somebody tell me which one got there quicker, Danny Conway or the ball?"

At times, it was hard for the other players to watch their catcher constantly berated this way. One day after practice, Coach O'Connor spoke with the head coach about Dan and reminded him that the kid was a very good player who had a real shot at getting drafted. If only for that reason, he suggested cutting the kid a little slack, and at some point saying something to build his confidence back up just so that he knows he's okay, or at least not terrible.

Hickey didn't say anything to O'Connor then, but later they were at Brad's together. It was getting late. The students were starting to arrive. The coaches paid their tab and left. As they were walking around the corner, they passed Dan and some of the other players. Coach Hickey saw them, but didn't look at them. He didn't say anything, either. He didn't have to.

Coach O'Connor did look at Dan. He looked him right in the eyes and shook his head.

Dan had not actually been to Brad's since the previous fall, and for the Friars' starting catcher the timing for a visit could not have been worse. His absence, though, was not by choice, and he had only recently returned after being expelled indefinitely from the public drinking establishment for something he did early on as a freshman. The penalty Dan had served earned him a notable and dubious distinction which his teammates never fail to bring up at every opportunity, so it would be remiss not to mention it here. Unofficially, he is still regarded as the only PC baseball player ever banned from Brad's. The infraction; urinating in the storage room. Dan had claimed that the line for the men's room was too long and he couldn't wait. But freshmen are not easily pardoned and his banishment lasted a full year.

CHAPTER 7   WINTER IN PROVIDENCE

UNDER THE KNIFE

As the fall season came to an end and December approached, it seemed like it had been two years instead of two months since the players had learned that this season would be everyone's last in a Friar uniform. The experience helped them gel. They grew as individuals and a team, becoming a family. Though it was a bond that was formed quickly, it would last a lifetime. But none of them were thinking about anywhere near that far in advance. In fact, none of them were looking beyond the middle of May and where they would finish in the conference. The true visionaries were contemplating June, and how far they would get in the Division I playoffs. A couple of big injuries, however, threatened the dreams and promise held for the 1999 Friars baseball season.

Staff ace, Marc DesRoches, began experiencing a sharp pain in his pitching elbow along with numbness and weakness in his fingers and hand. He was immediately shut down and there was speculation that the team might lose him for the season. Also, sophomore pitcher Mike Stuart's left shoulder had been bothering him most of the fall. Stewy didn't say anything at first, in part because he had never had any real arm trouble before and it was new to him. He also had not done much throwing that season, but he finally brought his balky shoulder to the attention of the coaching staff as the fall schedule was concluding. It was his first visit to the training room for an injury, and he didn't know what to expect.

The impression he was given was that it was not a serious problem, but they scheduled an appointment with a specialist, anyway, just to be certain. So for a few weeks, Stewy had to sweat it out. While the injury did not appear to be as severe as Marc's, the young lefty feared that he, too, might miss the 1999 campaign.

Stewy had an impact on the team the previous year as a freshman, and he knew he was being counted on in '99 to help Providence make their final season one to remember. The Friars were looking for a top lefty reliever, and he was in the mix. It would be terribly disappointing for him if he had to undergo surgery and miss any portion of the season.

John Rock was the athletic trainer and Assistant Athletic Director of Sports Medicine at the college. He began working with Stewy, having the young pitcher stretch and perform various exercises to strengthen the shoulder joint. He also utilized other forms of treatment that included electrical muscle stimulation, ultrasound and hot and cold compresses.

In early December, both Stewy and Marc went to see an orthopedic surgeon together. Coach Hickey and John Rock made the visit with them. In Stewy's case, the doctor didn't find any structural damage, as had been expected. He was prescribed rest, taking as much time off from throwing as was needed. Stewy was given an okay to continue the regiment of strengthening exercises and treatment. He was also given a cortisone shot to reduce some of the swelling. Stewy left the surgeon's office ecstatic. With the season a couple months away, it left him plenty of time to heal and get his strength back before opening day.

Marc's injury, however, proved to be quite a bit more serious. It was confirmed that the source of Marc's pain and numbness was due to an impingement of the ulnar nerve in the elbow. This is the same nerve that shocks and numbs your hand and arm when you hit your elbow on something hard. It is commonly known as the "funny bone." There were two options available for Marc. The non-invasive, conservative treatment called for completely stopping the activity that was causing the symptoms for an extended period and then slowly begin an exercise program to gradually stretch and strengthen the forearm muscles. With this approach, he would miss the entire season. The alternative, of course, was surgery. He would be looking at two to three months recovery time, though the range would depend entirely on Marc. The best possible scenario would have him ready for opening day, but there was also the very real possibility that he might never pitch again.

Patient, doctor and coach all agreed that, given the circumstances, immediate surgery was the best option. The procedure Marc underwent was ulnar nerve transposition, and it was performed a couple weeks later by Dr. Arthur Pappas, who was also the team physician for the Boston Red Sox. The goal of surgery was to release the pressure on the ulnar nerve where it passes through the cubital tunnel. The operation involved the surgeon forming a completely new tunnel from the flexor muscles of the forearm. The ulnar nerve was then moved out of the cubital tunnel and placed in the new tunnel. It was outpatient surgery that used general anesthesia, and when Marc came out of it there was no way of knowing how his elbow would respond. Everyone knew he would work his butt off, a few thought he would be able to get back to where he was before the surgery, but no one predicted that he would have a career year, leading the Friars baseball team to what would arguably be their best season in the history of the school.

PARTY LIKE IT'S 1999

While the team had the week off before the Christmas break to prepare for final exams, a lot of players broke up the monotony of studying the same way as the other students. There were plenty of parties on and off campus. Whether it was visiting local bars or partying in the dorms late into the night, there was no shortage of beer, bad judgment and alcohol-courage.

One night, Stewy was out with some of the boys and a friend from his hometown who had come down from Canton, MA. His shoulder, and the rest of him, was feeling pretty good until a fight broke out around him. Stewy almost couldn't help getting caught up in the fracas and ended up hurting his pitching hand pretty badly.

Stewy and his buddy, along with roommates Dan Conway and Mike "Scooter" Scott, as well as some other friends from school, had all gone to Prime Time, a local club, to throw back a few beers. There were a bunch of other baseball players present, as well as some PC hockey players, who were all hanging out together. An argument erupted between a group of guys and some of the athletes. There was one guy in the group who was pretty drunk and vocal, just looking to pick a fight. Earlier that night, Stewy happened to be standing next to the guy and made an attempt to calm him down by informing him that he and his friends were greatly outnumbered. Without being confrontational,

Stewy cautioned him that pursing a fight was not a good idea. The guy actually thanked him for the warning and the night continued. Stewy didn't see the guy again and that seemed to be the end of it. Then, as the bar was closing and everyone was leaving, he ran into the guy, who was even more drunk by this point. He started yelling at Stewy for no reason and calling him a pussy. The guy was convinced that Stewy had done something wrong by him. The sophomore pitcher reminded him that he had intervened earlier trying to keep the peace, but the guy wouldn't listen. He persisted, instigating a fight.

A tight circle of onlookers formed around the two of them as the confrontation escalated. There was going to be a fight, there was no question about it at this point. Before the guy had a chance to throw the first punch, Stewy made a move to get in position to fight when he tripped over someone's feet. As he was falling to the ground, the other guy responded by throwing a wild haymaker. To those watching it looked like the punch landed and knocked Stewy down, but it had completely missed him. On the floor, Stewy grabbed the guy's legs so he couldn't kick him and then wrestled him to the ground. Stewy managed to scramble atop the combatant and began to unload a barrage of punches, his arms flailing away, not sure what he was hitting. The other guy curled up in a defensive position and never got in a single punch. Stewy, in a blind fury, didn't realize that he had broken a bone in his pitching hand. When the pain finally registered, he let up and knew right away that something was wrong. Mad at himself for breaking his hand on this guy's head, he punched him a few more times for good measure. Then his buddies stepped in and pulled him off the bloodied drunk to get him out of there before the cops arrived. He got into his friend's car and they drove back to campus with the sirens approaching in the distance.

Stewy woke up the next morning with a hand the size of a catcher's mitt. He went straight to the hospital to have it evaluated. He was thinking that he had shattered his whole hand, as well as his chances of pitching that year. X-rays revealed only a small break, but he still had to tell Coach Hickey what happened.

Because of the swelling, a soft cast was applied to his hand and the whole thing was wrapped in heavy bandages. He left the hospital, dreading what he had to do next.

Coach Hickey was in his office, the door wide open when Stewy knocked weakly on the door frame with his right hand. He took one step inside and stopped.

The coach looked up from what he was doing, glanced at the dressing on his hand and then peered into the eyes of his sophomore pitcher. "What happened?"

It was almost as if he already knew, but he wanted to hear it from his player directly.

Stewy didn't walk any further inside. "We were all out last night and there was this guy…"

Coach Hickey interrupted him immediately. "I'm not sure if I heard you right, but if you said *we*, I am going to make you tell me who you were with."

"Umm, I was out last night at a bar," he began again, and as he told the story, Coach Hickey continually shook his head and called him an idiot several times. When he finished, the coach shook his head and called him an idiot one more time.

"That was just about as stupid a thing as you could possibly do," he said. "You have a sore shoulder that you're rehabbing, with the season just around the corner, and this is what you do. What the hell were you thinking? Don't answer. Just go. Get the hell out of my sight until you're serious about playing baseball and not acting like an idiot."

Stewy left without saying another word. He took his finals with a broken hand, but took off the soft cast so he could write. After exams, a hard cast was applied to the injured paw. During the Christmas break, he would drive down to PC from Canton, MA to work with the trainer.

GROUNDHOG DAY

As snow began falling on the city in regular accumulations and Trinity Rep continued performing its holiday tradition with an ever-changing stage production of Dickens' *A Christmas Carol*, there was little activity around the Providence College campus.

With a month-long semester break from books and baseball, many of the Friar ballplayers were looking forward to taking time off to spend with family and friends over the holidays. There was no formal exercise or weightlifting plan for the team to follow over the Christmas vacation, but most of the guys worked out on their own. Although the dorms on campus were officially closed, the Baseball House was always open.

There were a few players around campus during the break. Jeremy Sweet and Keith Reed were there working with Coach Hickey on a baseball camp for younger kids. Stewy came down to work a few days with the kids as well, volunteering his time as part of his atonement for being an idiot. He wanted to show the coach, and the team, that he was going to work hard to get ready for the season. He did a lot of running inside the sports complex. When he finally got the hard cast off, the other players started coming back and he began to throw a little. To his grave disappointment, he immediately discovered that his shoulder wasn't feeling any better so another MRI was scheduled. At that point, there wasn't much else he could do except wait for the results to come back. And run. That's what he did. He would test out his arm every day before practice, hoping that would be the day he was pain-free.

The team started out practicing indoors, but as early February came around, if there was no snow on the ground, the team would go outside, it didn't matter the temperature.

Coach Hickey was by no means sympathetic to the players with injuries who sat out the morning outdoor conditioning sessions because of subfreezing temperatures. He was a New Englander. It was where he was born. He played and coached his entire life in winter weather. He would say, "I'm sick and tired of hearing 'my leg hurts,' 'my back hurts,' 'my pussy hurts.'"

Then one day in mid February, just before the trip to Florida, it was warm enough to go outside and have a regular practice, on real grass and dirt. Stewy gave throwing another chance, and to his surprise he found that his shoulder actually felt pretty good. He excitedly told Coach O'Connor, who told him he could play some long toss but not to push it and see how the shoulder responded. From that point on his shoulder was fine. He would make the trip to Florida with the team and be ready to contribute to the historic PC baseball season.

CHAPTER 8   PROVIDENCE COLLEGE

A BRIEF HISTORY

Providence College was founded in 1917 through a joint effort of the Roman Catholic Diocese of Providence and the Dominican Friars of the Province of St. Joseph. Two years later, an inaugural class of 71 male students was instructed by 19 Dominican faculty members. PC remains the only institution for higher learning in the country that is administered by the Order of Dominican Preachers. The school adopted the motto "Veritas," meaning truth, from the goddess of the same name in Roman mythology.

Located less than two miles northwest of downtown Providence, the campus has continued to expand through the years from its original 17-acres to more than a hundred and five. Sitting atop Smith Hill, the highest point of the capitol city, are twenty-one academic and administrative buildings, nine dormitories, six suite-style apartment buildings, five Dominican residences, three athletic buildings, as well as six outdoor athletic facilities, including a new "turf field."

Competing for enrollment numbers with four other major colleges in the city of Providence alone, among them Brown University and Rhode Island School of Design, PC holds its own. Known for its programs in the liberal arts and sciences, it offers its approximately 4,000 undergraduate and 1,000 graduate students a choice of fifty majors and twenty-four minors.

Providence College remained an all-male institution until 1971, when it opened its doors to women. Six years later, one of the darkest hours in the college's history occurred. In the early morning hours of December 13, 1977, with final exam grades weighing heavily on the minds of many students, some female residents of Aquinas Hall organized a floor party to celebrate the end of the semester and their efforts in a campus-wide Christmas decoration contest. Following a snowball fight that lasted late into the night, the female students came back into the old building and began drying themselves off with hairdryers. Then, tragedy struck when faulty wiring in Room 405 began to throw sparks out of two outlets, generating a flame. The Christmas decorations quickly ignited and fueled a fire which spread rapidly up and down the hall. Although the blaze was completely extinguished with forty-five minutes, ten female students died as a result of the fire. Four lost their lives due to smoke inhalation, four died from burns they suffered in the conflagration and two others were killed when they jumped out of fourth floor windows of Aquinas Hall before firefighters could reach them by ladder. Today, on the brick facing along the front of Aquinas Hall, there is a plaque commemorating the ten young women who were lost in this disaster.

Through the years, Providence College has produced many notable alumni from all walks of life. In the political arena, graduates include U.S. House of Representative, Patrick Kennedy, United States Senator Christopher Dodd, Lieutenant Governor Charles Fogarty and former Boston Mayor, Raymond Flynn. In the business world, Arthur Ryan, chairman and CEO of Prudential Insurance Company was a 1963 Providence College graduate. Elizabeth Flynn Lott, former Executive Vice President of J.P. Morgan Chase and Company came out of PC's 1982 class.

In the entertainment field, film director Peter Farrelly, comedienne Janeane Garofalo and actor John O'Hurley, of *Seinfeld's* Mr. Peterman-fame, were all PC graduates.

FRIAR ATHLETICS

Sports at Providence College have always been a big part of the school's lore. PC's sports teams are called the Friars, after the Dominican Catholic Order that runs the school. They are the only collegiate team to use the name. All teams participate in the NCAA's Division I and in the Big East Conference, except for the Men's and Women's hockey programs, which compete in Hockey East, and the Men's Lacrosse program, which competes in the MAAC. Teams which participate in the Big East Conference include the men's and women's basketball team, men's and women's cross country, field hockey, men's and women's soccer, softball, men's and women's swimming and diving, women's tennis, men's and women's track and field and women's volleyball.

Current and former professional athletes in many sports were one-time Friars. The very successful men's basketball program boasts more players who have gone on to play in the NBA than any other pro sport by a wide margin. The list of names is impressive, and includes Austin Croshere, Eric Williams, Ryan Gomes, Marvin Barnes, Otis Thorpe, Ernie DiGregorio, Kevin Stacom, Jimmy Walker, Joe Hassett, player-coach Lenny Wilkens, longtime Georgetown Hoyas coach John Thompson, Florida Gators coach Billy Donovan as well as Rich Gotham, president of the Boston Celtics.

In 1961 the Friar basketball team won their first title in the NIT (National Invitational Tournament), arguably the national championship in those years, behind the leadership of senior guard, Lenny Wilkens. Providence basketball took home its second NIT championship in 1963, led that year by John Thompson.

In 1971, when Providence College began admitting women and enrollment nearly doubled, almost instantly PC basketball tickets became a hot commodity at the cramped Alumni Hall Gymnasium. With the opening of the Providence Civic Center in 1972, the Friars conveniently moved downtown and had a magical season. The men's basketball team advanced to the Final Four in the 1972-1973 season on the play and leadership of Providence natives Ernie DiGregorio and Marvin Barnes, while the women's basketball team played their inaugural season in Alumni Hall.

Providence's influence on college athletics was further marked with the creation of the Big East Conference in 1979 by Dave Gavitt, the men's basketball coach, and later with the establishment of the Hockey East conference in 1983 by the men's hockey coach, Lou Lamoriello. During this time, the PC student body changed drastically, when for the first time women outnumbered men in incoming classes and non-Rhode Island students outnumbered instate Friars.

Also in 1983, the lady Friars basketball team won their first-ever Big East Tournament. Notable alumni on that team include Doris Burke, who later became an ESPN basketball commentator.

Men's basketball again took center stage on the Providence campus as Coach Rick Pitino and senior guard Billy Donovan took the Friars to their second Final Four appearance in 1987. Overall, the Friars have had fifteen NCAA basketball tournament berths and sixteen NIT berths, as well as twenty-four basketball All-Americans.

Basketball has always been the darling of all the men's sports programs at Providence College. And with very good reason. They've had a lot of success through the years, gaining a national reputation as a perennial Big East contender and turning out some of the best talent in the sport, both on the court and on the sidelines.

The hockey program also garners its fair share of attention from the student body as well as the school administration, at least in terms of operating budgets, recruiting and scholarships. The men's hockey team played their first season in their new home on campus, Schneider Arena, in 1973. The arena still houses the skating Friars as well as intramural college games and local youth leagues. The men's hockey team has won two Hockey East titles and two ECAS titles. They have been in the NCAA Division I hockey tournament ten times, their best finish in the tournament being national runner-up in 1985. The men's hockey team has produced several NHL players as well as coaches and general managers, including Chris Terreri, a longtime NHL standout goalie.

BASEBALL TRADITION

The list of Friar baseball players who went on to play in the pros might be more modest, but the school produced as many major leaguers during the 1990's as it did in the first 70 years of the program's existence.

In 1920, Providence's first athletic competition was a baseball game against Rhode Island School of Design. In that decade, Providence produced three players who made it all the way to the Bigs, including former Boston Red Sox catcher, Birdie Tebbetts. In the baseball program's final decade, three more players went all the way, including Lou Merloni and John McDonald.

Of the four "major" sports, football was the first program to be eliminated. Before the team was disbanded in the early 1970s due to dwindling attendance and budget, they played all their homes games on Hendricken Field. Perhaps the best sibling rivalry analogy to describe the three remaining major sports at PC would be to use the Brady sisters from the 1970's TV show, *The Brady*

Bunch. In this correlation, basketball would be the enviable and much sought-after Marsha, while hockey could be likened to the cute if easily dismissed Cindy and baseball was the embodiment of the ugly duckling and summarily ignored middle sister, Jan.

Athletes who came to Providence to play baseball certainly understand this. It's the way it was. They knew that the stands of Hendricken Field were not going to be filled, the games would not be broadcast on television and they would not hear cheerleaders calling out their names. None of that. They would be practicing outside on frozen fields in the winter and on muddy infields and damp grass in the spring. They would help prepare the field for play, raking out rocks and filling in holes that were missed by the school's groundskeepers. The baseball players were not given all that much considering the Division I program they competed in. There were about seven scholarships available, but no one got a free ride and the money was split among the twenty-five or so players. And they were hardly spoiled with the facilities at the college. They did not expect much and they did not complain, even when they were given old lockers that were hand-me-downs from the basketball team a generation before. In 1999, Marvin Barnes' name was still imprinted in old tape on one of them. The facilities at every school they traveled to were far superior to their own at home, including the high schools fields they visited in Florida during the spring. The baseball players, however, would gladly have put up with playing under these conditions if their sport had not been eliminated. They would have continued to buy their own gear and equipment. They would do all these things because they loved the game. That was the only reason. Most of the kids who put on a PC baseball uniform from 1920-1999 did it because they just wanted to play the game they loved.

In more recent years, several sports programs, both men's and women's, have enjoyed success on the playing field. Cross country might arguably be the school's most successful sports program. They have participated in the NCAA championships 17 straight years through 2005. Keith Kelley, 2000, was the first Friar to win the individual national cross country championship. And it was the women's cross country team that won Providence's only national championship in 1996. Kim Smith, 2005, became the first Friar woman to win the individual national championship in the sport.

The women's hockey team has consistently been one of the best in the country. In the 1998 Winter Olympics in Nagano, Japan, seven members of the gold-medal winning U.S. Women's Ice Hockey team were Providence College alumni or current Friars.

But in 1999, it would be the baseball team that would make their mark in PC history.

PART II. THE FINAL SEASON

Don't tell me about the world. Not today. It's springtime and they're knocking baseballs around fields where the grass is damp and green in the morning and the kids are trying to hit the curve ball.

-Pete Hamill, American Author

CHAPTER 9 "PLAY BALL!"

SEASONS IN THE SUN

Baseball in New England is often played in weather that is more suited for football. Rain, snow, sleet, freezing rain, hail, anything that mother nature can throw at you, she does. It's not at all unusual for a late season winter storm, or even an entire week of spring rain to postpone multiple games, so double-headers become a way of life in Big East Baseball.

Getting practices in between games during the season is challenging enough, so the annual trip that the team makes to Florida each winter is always welcome. To start the year, PC's schedule is typically heavy with non-conference games against schools in the south. They would usually play about a dozen games over a two-week period from the last week of February through the first week of March, including games in the southern Florida city of Homestead, where the Friars call home during this time. This year, the Friars were scheduled to open up the season with a weekend series against the College of Charleston in South Carolina, playing two doubleheaders before returning home for a week of practice and preparation for their extended southern trip.

MAKING THE GRADE

That February, PC third baseman Angelo Ciminiello, was named Big East Scholar Athlete Of The Year, earning a $4,000 postgraduate scholarship as part of the award. When Providence's Gladys Ganiel, a female distance runner, won the women's award, it was only the second time in Big East history that one school won both awards. Angelo also won PC's Vincent McAndrew Award as senior athlete with the top GPA (3.73 in biology/pre-med). With the goal of becoming a heart surgeon, he had already been accepted by three medical schools, including the prestigious Jefferson Medical College in Philadelphia. Though he realized his dream of becoming a professional baseball player was a long shot, he epitomized the All-American scholar-athlete ideal. For Angelo, his success on the field and in the classroom were not mutually exclusive. One played off the other, and he found that he was able to manage his time more efficiently if he was busy, doing the things he really enjoyed.

That same week during practice, Angelo rolled his ankle during practice, just days before the start of the regular season. Fortunately, it was only a sprain, but it would require time to heal, and he would miss the season opening series. Freshman, Brendan Trainor would be given third base duties in Angelo's absence.

Adding to the injury woes of the Friars that pre-season was a wrist sprain to junior, Jason Hairston. It was more of a nagging pain than an injury, the variety that may not cause him to miss any time, but the kind that could persist the whole season and limit production, and consequently playing time, which would be unfortunate for the speedy outfielder who had broken into the starting lineup in 1998, batting .333 in Big East Games.

There was no way of knowing it at the time, but Jason's injury would open the door for another player, Mike Scott, allowing him to evolve and become a major contributor to the team's success that year. When Scooter got his chance to play, he would take complete advantage of it. After sitting out the entire 1998 season due to a knee injury, the minute he was inserted into the lineup and began playing every day he got hot and stayed hot, leaving Coach Hickey with little choice but to continue to play the sophomore phenom. Jason would take his diminished playing time in stride, knowing it would help the team. He would simply assume the role that had been carved out for him, a late inning defensive replacement, who would always to ready when called upon, and when he had a chance to get an at-bat late in the game he remained focused and able to contribute. If he needed to give himself up with a bunt or a ground ball to the right side to move a runner over, that's what he would be committed to do, not try to win back his job by swinging for the fences and making up for lost at-bats.

GOOD START

With the season set to begin, the Friars would go with who they had available and play through their injuries, as all teams must. Depth was what every team needs to win, and that was one of the strengths Providence had going into the season. It would be put to the test early.

In the northeast, winter still held sway as the Friars opened their regular season in South Carolina with four games in two days against the College of Charleston Cougars. On February 20, the first game of Providence's historic final season, Josh Burnham was given the ball and he pounded the strike zone in a hard-fought 5-4 Friars victory. He pitched all seven innings – the number of innings played in a scheduled double-header – with a gutsy, bend-but-not-break effort. The ten hits he allowed were twice as many as his offense managed. Scooter had a single, a double and 2 RBI.

In the second game that day, Stork pitched 6.2 innings of shutout ball, scattering 5 hits as the Friars edged the Cougars again, this time 1-0. Like all the other players, Stork wore his "THERE'S ONLY ONE THING LEFT TO DO..." T-shirt under his uniform. It replaced the one his mother made for him the year before featuring an image of a hand gripping a baseball and "STORK" in cursive lettering underneath. He wore that every game the previous season. This year, his personal identity took a backseat to a more selfless, team-concept approach to under-uniform attire. Offensively for the Friars, Scooter collected two more hits in this game and scored the only run of the contest on a sacrifice fly by Mike O'Keefe.

The two teams met again for a pair the following day. The result was a couple more close games. The first featured PC's big right-hander, Rob Corraro, going the distance in the 5-3 win. Providence benefited from nine walks from opposing pitchers and Scooter collected two more hits, scoring twice and driving in a run.

Angelo tested his ankle during the game and the results were not encouraging. He aggravated the ankle after striking out in his only at-bat and left the game.

In the second game, freshman Ryan Lewis got collared in the 4-2 loss. The young lefty, however, showed that he had the temperament, as well as the sense of humor, to endure the challenge of dealing with the adversity of a rough start. After struggling through the first inning, he stepped into the dugout and began walking along the bench, lifting up gloves and towels and kicking around bags. Few players even noticed him, but one who did was Stork. He watched Ryan for a while as he walked back and forth, obviously looking for something.

"Ry, what are you doing?" Stork asked.

Ryan turned to him and said, "I lost my curveball. Have you seen my curveball anywhere? If it turns up, let me know. I could use it." And then he continued on looking around the dugout as if he were expecting to find it. Some of the guys who heard the exchange just smiled and shook their head. Stork couldn't help but laugh himself.

Taking three of four games was a good way to start the season, but the weekend victories came with a price; another injury. Freshman outfielder/pitcher, Brendan Ryan, broke his wrist when he ran into the fence shagging fly balls during BP between games on Sunday. He got one at-bat in the first game and walked before he was lost for the season.

Watching the young player walking off the field with the athletic trainer and holding his wrist, Coach Hickey shook his head and said, "Stupid things happen to stupid people."

CALLING IT QUITS

In contrast to freshman southpaw Ryan Lewis's carefree approach to the game, and life, was senior Josh Cox, who had been called upon to pitch in relief of the kid from southern California. When he did not pitch effectively, contributing to the team's first loss of the season, the righty from Cambridge, Massachusetts reached a personal crossroad and decided to quit. It was no whim, but something he had been considering for awhile, and now his failure out of the bullpen convinced him it was time to hang it up. He was seeing his friends really enjoying their last semester of college, planning trips for Spring Break while he rode the pine. He certainly didn't need to stick it out only to hurt the team by getting lit up when he got into a game.

As a freshman, Josh not only made the team as a walk-on player, but he actually got a decent amount of playing time, which is not an easy thing to do. Most every other player had been recruited, so in order to take time away from them you *had* to be impressive. Players such as Josh sometimes never get a chance to play, and when they do, if they don't do something good with that opportunity they may never get another one. This kind of pressure makes it even more difficult for players like Josh to perform, yet he did what he was supposed to do every time out, knowing full well that each pitch that missed its mark and was hit out of the park could be his last, and then he would be keeping track of pitch counts for Coach O'Connor or throwing BP.

Like any competitive athlete, Josh had certain expectations for himself. In his first two years, after proving himself reliable, a pitcher able to come in out of the bullpen and throw strikes, a torn labrum caused him to sit out his entire junior year to rehab his right shoulder. Josh worked hard to come back in 1999, but he was never quite the same. His velocity was down and his curveball lost its bite. Still, he thought he would be able to work through it and be able to perform well each time out.

Shortly after the team returned to Providence, Josh went to see Coach Hickey in his office before practice and told him he could not continue, that he lost the drive and lost his confidence in himself. The Coach listened to what Josh had to say, then he told his player that he would regret the decision. "This team is making history," he said, "and you have a chance to be a part of it." He asked Josh to take a few days to think about it before he handed in his uniform. Josh agreed, and when he got back out onto the practice field and saw how happy his buddies were to see him, it made him realize how much he enjoyed playing and being around the guys and he did not want to quit on himself or the team. At the end of the week, Josh had his bags packed and he traveled to Florida with his teammates, happy just to be there and contribute in whatever way he could.

HOMESTEAD ADVANTAGE

Playing at Hendricken Field in Providence at this time of the year was not an option, so the Friars played their next game as hosts to Northwood University at their winter training facility in Homestead, Florida on February 27.

Providence pounded out 18 hits in a lopsided 17-1 victory paced by Scooter, who had five knocks, and senior second baseman Paul Costello, who collected four. Jamie Athas contributed three, as did Keith Reed, two of which left the yard and were good for 6 RBI in the game.

Chris Caprio, another Friar who sat out the 1998 season, had his first at-bat of his baseball career. He walked and scored a run in the PC romp.

Lost in all the offense was the pitching performance by Marc DesRoches, fresh from elbow surgery. The big righty maintained good command of his pitches and threw them consistently for strikes. Though Marc may have lost some of his velocity, he had enough to punch out eight hitters as he moved the ball well around the plate. He went six innings, allowing only three hits along the way in earning his first win of the season.

The following day, the Friars opened up a two-game series with the University of Dayton in Homestead and suffered a ten inning setback, falling 8-6. Mike O'Keefe drove in three runs as he came a single away from hitting for the cycle. Josh Burnham pitched eight strong innings, allowing only three runs on seven hits and did not factor in the decision, as the bullpen let this one get away.

Angelo tested his ankle again, playing third and batting twice. However, when he began to experience pain and some swelling in the ankle he was taken out as a precaution. It had been a week since he last attempted to play, and Coach Hickey thought it would be best to have his third baseman sit out a couple more weeks to allow the ankle to heal properly, not wanting to have the injury linger and affect his play all season long.

The two teams went back at it on Monday, with the Friars' avenging the previous day's loss with a 7-6 victory over the Dayton Flyers. Rob Corraro did not have his best stuff, but supported by some timely Friar hitting, he managed to pick up his second win of the young season. Keith Reed sparked the offense with three hits, hitting his third homer of the season and driving in four.

GONE FISHIN'

Each year, a small percentage of PC's student body, traveling to South Florida for Spring Break, make the thirty mile commute from the Miami beaches to support the team and spend time in Homestead with the boys. Some of the players' parents also take flights down to escape the winter cold and watch their sons play baseball. This year, not surprisingly, there were more students and parents in Homestead than previous years. It's always a lot of fun for everyone, with much more going on than just baseball.

On the team's only day off which they didn't have to travel, a deep sea fishing trip had been organized by Coach O'Connor and Navvy, inviting anyone who wanted to go. They chartered two boats, which were very quickly filled with players, many of whom didn't know a thing about fishing. The boats were also filled with cases of ice cold beer. That, they knew what to do with. Naturally, everyone ended up pretty drunk.

Stork had to drive the van back to the hotel because he was pretty much the only player who hadn't been drinking. He had gotten used to being the designated driver the entire trip, as he had been entrusted to get team members back safely from a variety of south Florida establishments.

Some of the guys actually caught fish, which they cooked and ate when they got back, even though Coach Hickey insisted that everyone go out to dinner that night. Okie ended up hooking a barracuda and keeping it in the sink at the hotel.

RECORD-SETTING PACE

On March 3, the Friars were inhospitable hosts to St. Bonaventure, crushing the A-10 Conference team 20-2. Providence had 22 hits in the blowout, and everyone contributed. Neal McCarthy drove in six runs alone. Jeremy Sweet homered and had 4 RBI. Scooter had three more hits, hitting safely in all eight games on the season for the Friars at a ridiculous .559 clip.

It didn't matter how one-sided the game was, freshman Ryan Lewis couldn't contain his excitement as he was credited with his first college win. He went seven innings, K'ing nine Bonnies along the way.

The Friars took their 6-2 record with them to a second game that same day, visiting Florida International University, a nationally ranked team at #18. Marc DesRoches came in relief of Stork, who pitched well before running into trouble in 8th inning and allowing the Golden Panthers to tie the game. Marc got Stork, and the Friars, out of further trouble that inning, but surrendered a leadoff, walk-off 10th inning homerun and suffered what would be his only loss of the season as the Friars were defeated, 7-6. Scooter had two hits and Keith Reed slugged season homerun number four in a losing effort.

After a travel day, the team would bounce back in a big way and embark on a long winning streak that would last nearly three weeks and encompass fifteen games. They began the streak with a 15-3 win against St. Bonaventure in Homestead on March 5.

Josh Burnham improved to 2-0, allowing just one hit in seven innings of work while striking out eight. Keith Reed went 4-4 with a homerun and three RBI. Dan Conway had a perfect day, as well, going 3-3 with a walk and knocking in three. Jeremy Sweet also drove in three and Scooter continued his hot hitting, ten straight games now with a total of 23 hits.

The following day, Bucknell University became Providence's next victim, falling to the Friars 5-4. Rob Corraro won for the third time with another complete game effort. Though they were out hit by the visiting Pennsylvania school, the Friars got the hits when they needed them. The Bison, however, managed to do something that no team had been able to accomplish up to that point, and that was to hold PC's Mike Scott hitless for an entire game. Scooter's ten game hitting streak was snapped.

Providence closed out the southern portion of their travel schedule on March 7, hosting New York City's Wagner College. Behind the eight strong innings tossed by Marc DesRoches and an offensive attack that was sparked by three homeruns, the Friars left south Florida with a 14-2 victory over the Seahawks. Keith Reed hit his sixth jack of the season. Jeremy Sweet and Mike O'Keefe both connected for long balls as well, and Jamie Athas continued to impress, going 4-4 and knocking in three.

Keith Reed would be awarded Big East Player Of The Week honors, amassing 14 hits, four of them homeruns, in six games. For the same week, ending March 8, Scooter was named Rookie Of The Week for his consistent offensive production.

GETTING OUT OF TOWN

The last night in Florida, after the Wagner win, most of the guys went out to celebrate a successful road trip. They had three days before their next game, and Coach Hickey told them to go out and enjoy themselves, but to keep in mind that they had to be up to catch an early flight home in the morning.

Shuffling the guys around with Stork was Alan Segee, the team's trainer. Neither of them drank, so the two of them hung out quite a bit together that week. Stork and Alan had initially gotten close because they were both big movie fans, and films were something they talked about a lot. Alan had an encyclopedic knowledge when it came to Oscar trivia, and during many of the games, although Stork might have been on the opposite side of the bench working on a pitching chart, the two would play Six Degrees of Kevin Bacon between innings, giving each other three outs to come up with the answer. They did that all season, starting in the fall.

Stork and Alan had dropped the guys off at an area club and then went out to get something to eat. In the middle of dinner, Alan received a phone call from one of the coaches informing him that Josh Cox was in the hospital. He had developed a nasty case of food poisoning after eating at a burger joint earlier in the night.

Alan remembered that Josh was not among the players who had gone out that night. When his teammates decided to go clubbing, Josh wasn't feeling right and decided to stay behind. Shortly after, as he was overwhelmed by nausea and crippling stomach pain, he began throwing up. Since the players' van wasn't back yet, in between retches he went down to the hotel bar where he knew he would find the coaching staff. Josh asked if someone could drive him to the hospital to get checked out. The coaches took him immediately in their car.

Coach O'Connor made the call to Alan's cell phone, asking him to meet them at the hospital so he could take Josh back to the hotel. It would have been out of the way to drop Stork off first, so he went with Alan to the hospital.

In the emergency room, Josh had to wait a long time before he was seen, vomiting the entire time. He was finally diagnosed with a serious case of gastroenteritis, and ended up staying most of the night in the hospital with an IV in his arm.

Coach Hickey, O'Connor and Navvy were there, along with Joe Valenzano. While at the hospital together, Stork sat with Navvy and they talked for awhile. It was really the first time the two of them had ever said more than a couple words to each other in passing. Pitchers and hitting instructors don't usually cross paths very often, but Stork and Navvy got to know each other quite well from this time together. They talked a lot more after that and have remained close ever since.

While the coaches went back to the hotel in their car, Alan waited at the hospital for Josh to be discharged. Coach Hickey had asked the players to be outside the hotel by the buses and ready to leave for the airport by 7 a.m. Everyone was there, including Josh and Alan. They had just enough time to get back and pack their stuff. The only person who was not there at the arranged time was Coach Hickey. When one of the other coaches went to check on him they found him asleep in his room. Because they had to wait for him, the team missed their scheduled flight and had to fly separately, taking three different planes to get everyone home. Two groups made it back that day, but one didn't get into Providence until the following day.

CHAPTER 10   THE STREAK

HENDRICKEN FIELD

The Friars true home opener was scheduled for March 10, when they returned to Hendricken Field in Providence to host Central Connecticut. It would be the baseball team's final home opener in Providence College history, but it was almost postponed when a foot of snow fell on the field two nights before. The team learned something that week; they were in this alone. It was a lesson that certainly had already been taught, but it would become perfectly clear that the administration did not have their backs when Plumber and Coach Hickey were out on the plow clearing the snow and a school vice president had been sent over to throw them off the field.

And all year long, it was the same thing.

Whenever it rained – and it rained a lot that season – Coach Hickey would call down to what passed for the field's grounds crew in the morning before an afternoon game and inform them there was so many inches of standing water along the third base line or in front of the dugouts. The college didn't want to hear it, however. They would just as soon cancel the game before they would authorize to have any work done to the field. When nothing was done, the coach would contact Providence's Baseball Administrator and Senior Associate Athletic Director, Gerald "Jerry" Alaimo, who would in turn call Plumber, a guy that he knew could always be depended upon. Plumber would show up with pumps and hoses in hand and, with guys he pulled off his other plumbing jobs, pump the field dry so that the game could be played.

Like always, they got the field prepped on time. It was ready for opening day 1999 and baseball was played as scheduled. There was little pomp and circumstance, but the players were all up for it.

PRE-GAME ACTIVITIES

By this point of the season, the tradition that had been developed by Keith Reed over the time he had been at Providence had expanded, taking on a whole new life. Before each game, Keith would have the team form a circle around him and he would lead a pre-game huddle with everyone kind of jumping around him as he made up songs about all the guys on the team and things they had recently done, either on the field or off. While these antics were nothing new, this year it was much more pronounced, louder and more animated, and Jeremy Sweet was right there, leading the charge.

For all that Jeremy could do on the field, in the dugout no one could touch him, but everyone could hear him. He had a real flair for jawing at the opposing team, particularly the pitchers. From the moment their toes touched the rubber, he would be on them. Jeremy would yell things like, *"We're gonna own you all day," "You keep bringing that shit," "We got your number," "Put an L-screen up," "It's all BP from here on out."*

Jason Hairston, Coley O'Donnell and Mike O'Keefe usually got in on it, too. They were trying to get the pitchers to look at them. It became a game within a game among these Friars to see who could say something that would get the pitcher to look over, because once he did they would get even louder, more hostile. After a while, the pitchers would wisely avert their eyes from the Friar dugout altogether. Once they got into a pitcher's head, they would stay on him the entire game. Even the Friars who didn't participate in the chirping or who didn't much appreciate it, they all had each other's backs. It got to the point where other teams did not enjoy pitching against Providence, and not just because they were a very good hitting team with something to prove. Every one of them was into every single pitch of every inning of every game all season long. The dugout became their secret weapon. Not only would they try to beat a team between the lines, but they would also try to beat them mentally.

Being in the game this way was essential for Jeremy. Because his role was usually DH, spot starts at first base and pinch hitting, he had to remain sharp and focused when he wasn't playing defense. Jeremy had nicknames for all his teammates. He was called "Sweet Butters," though the opposition had plenty of other names for him that they thought suited him better.

Some of the teams Providence played that year thought they were all just a bunch of pricks. Others may have considered that kind of behavior unsportsmanlike, but the 1999 Friars were amped up on a high level of emotional energy, which they managed to sustain the entire season. They also made a lot of positive noise, cheering each other on vehemently during the games. They were looking for any advantage to help them win and they were having a lot of fun doing it. That was the key to everything. If some of the teams didn't like the way they played, it was too bad. After 1999, they wouldn't have to worry about it.

HOMECOMING 1999

Stork was the Friars' unlikely starter for the home opener, but the sophomore lefty tossed a complete game shutout with an inspired 100-pitch performance, allowing just two hits all afternoon. Brendan Trainor, who had been playing well filling in for Angelo at third, clubbed a two-run homer in the Friars 7-0 victory. Second baseman Paul Costello had a pair of hits and scored three times.

The players were ecstatic to come away with a win that day, though the historic significance of the event had little time to sink in with the team as they immediately went back on the road. They visited the University of Delaware on March 12 to open a three game series. Behind Josh Burnham's complete game performance, the Friars defeated the Blue Hens 9-4. Josh threw 141 pitches and improved to a perfect 3-0 on the season. Mike O'Keefe and Neal McCarthy homered for Providence, who won their last five games.

The next day the teams played two more, with the Friars taking both games of the double-header by scores of 2-1 and 18-6 respectively. In game one, Marc threw all seven innings in earning his third win of the season. Jeremy Sweet lashed two doubles, driving in one run and scoring the other. The game also marked Angelo's return to the lineup, and his first hit of the season was a double that drove in Jeremy with the go-ahead run in the top of the sixth inning.

The second game was one big highlight reel for Providence. Senior right-hander, Rob Corraro notched his fourth win without a defeat. On the other side of the ball, a twenty-hit attack was led by rookie sensation Jamie Athas, who collected five of the hits. Keith Reed drove in five and Mike Scott homered in the Friars' win.

Feeling no adverse affects in his ankle from playing in the first game, Angelo went back out to third in game two. He doubled in five plate appearances and then Brendan Trainor took over to give the co-captain a little rest in the blowout victory. The freshman singled in his only at bat and drove in a run. With Angelo's return, Brendan knew that his playing time would be greatly diminished, but he could hold his head high having performed well in the three weeks he had filled in for Angelo, making the plays at third and getting on base.

Jamie Athas shared Big East Rookie Of The Week honors for how he handled the stick.

EXTENDED HOMESTAND

Looking ahead at the schedule, the Friars had fourteen games in the next two weeks, all but two of which would be at Hendricken Field. They were already playing with a lot of confidence, and being at home for any length of time was a luxury and an advantage. The Friars were riding a seven game win-streak, when snow canceled their March 15 match up at Central Connecticut and threatened to slow their momentum. Providence didn't miss a beat, however, defeating Quinnipiac 9-7 back at home on St. Patrick's Day to make it eight in a row. A quality start by Ryan Lewis, who pitched effectively for seven innings, was almost blown by the bullpen. But the Friars prevailed behind a balanced offensive attack that preserved the win for Ryan. Scooter and Keith had three hits apiece and Okie drove in three with a bases loaded double early in the game.

The Irish holiday celebration began immediately after the game, with many of the players going straight over to Bradley Café in their uniforms. Despite having to play the following afternoon, they continued what they started at Brad's, shifting over to The Baseball House for an after-hours party. It must have been just what the team needed, because the Friars rolled over Sacred Heart University the next day at Hendricken Field, 27-6.

Right-handed senior Josh Cox posted his only win of the season in what would be his only start, working through five tough innings. It wasn't a great outing by any means, but it was a gutsy performance and a "W" for him and the team. The moment Josh threw his last pitch of the afternoon he knew Coach Hickey had been right. He was glad he hadn't quit. He would have regretted denying himself the opportunity to contribute to the 1999 Friars' season. It was the best second chance Josh had ever been given and he would always be grateful to Coach Hickey.

That day, however, the Friars' offense was the real story of the game. They pounded out 25 hits, including four homeruns. One of Neal McCarthy's four hits that day sailed over the fence, accounting for three of his five RBI. Angelo hit a two run shot and a grand slam. Coley O'Donnell hit the other tater. Okie didn't homer, but he had five hits, including two triples and a double and scored four times for the Friars, who won their ninth straight game and improved their overall record to 15-3.

The Friars' homestand and their winning ways continued over the weekend, when the Black Bears from Maine meandered down I-95 to play four games in two days at Hendricken Field. The visitors would head back north on Sunday night with four loses after Providence completed the sweep. 7-3 and 13-12 were the scores of Saturday's victories, and 10-4 and 9-3 on Sunday. The Friars Big Three, Marc, Josh and Rob all posted victories, and the Friar offense was clicking on all cylinders, smashing eight homeruns over the weekend series.

In the first game on Saturday, the Friars coasted to a victory behind Marc DesRoches complete game/eight strikeout performance. Neal McCarthy homered twice and Scooter went yard for Providence.

In the second game, the Friars were leading 8-7 after eight innings when the visiting team put a five-spot on the board in the top of the 9th. When the Friars came to bat in the home half of the ninth, facing a 12-8 deficit, they had plenty of life left, both in the batter's box and on the bench. Jeremy had a tough time at the plate that day, striking out three times for the hat trick. He knew he would be pinch hit for if his turn came up. He was coming up fourth that inning, so either way there would be no golden sombrero for him. Jeremy took a seat on the bench but his afternoon was far from over. He started in on the pitcher as he was taking his warm up tosses, and when Mike O'Keefe singled to open up the inning he became even more vocal. When the next batter, Angelo, homered, more Friars joined Jeremy, raising the decibel level of the chatter and forcing something to happen.

Three consecutive singles plated a third run, and suddenly it was 12-11. There was one out when Scooter came up with the tying and winning runs on base. A fresh arm, a lefty, was brought in to face Scooter, who did what he had been doing since the season began; he tripled and gave the Friars a thrilling walk-off win. PC sophomore, Brett Donovan, who pitched to one batter in the ninth and recorded a strike out, got credited with the win. It would be his first and only victory of the season.

After two more triumphs against Maine on Sunday, with Rob Corraro and Josh Burnham tossing complete games victories, just like that the win streak was up to thirteen.

Mike O'Keefe was the Big East Player Of The Week, while Scooter garnered Rookie Of The Week honors for their gaudy offenses performances.

The long homestand was interrupted briefly on March 23 when the Friars traveled to the University of Massachusetts, though the result was the same. Ryan Lewis went the distance and struck out nine in posting his third victory of the season, a 13-6 drubbing of the Minutemen. The sixteen-hit Friar attack included nine extra base hits, three of which were homeruns. Dan Conway hit a three-run blast, Okie and Angelo went back-to-back in the seventh. Afterward, it was right back home again for six games in five days.

With their confidence sky high, Providence hosted the University of Rhode Island on March 24. Among state rivals, this was the biggest. With a long winning streak on the line, the last thing the players wanted to do was have it snapped by URI. It was a raw, stormy day. A steady drizzle was falling and the poor field conditions at the start of the game gradually became worse. PC jumped out to an early lead, their first four batters in the lineup scoring, and the Friars prevailed 8-4 in a rain-shortened game, getting though the visitor's half of the seventh before it was called. Despite five errors behind him, sophomore lefty Mike Stuart picked up his first win of the season. It was a much closer game than it appeared, and it was one that everyone wanted to win, including Coach Hickey. He made it a point to drum home just how important the game was to the young lefty when he approached him between innings after URI scored a run in the 3rd to close the gap to 4-2. Stewy was talking to his parents at the backstop when Coach Hickey said, "You have no balls. And you're the reason they're back in this game." Then he walked away.

Stewy thought he had been pitching a pretty good game, though he had gotten some balls up in the zone the previous inning, allowing a few hard hits and surrendering an unearned run. He settled down after that, getting into the seventh inning before another error got him into further trouble and Scott Swanjord was called in to close the game.

Keith Reed cracked his eighth homer of the season in the victory and Scooter was perfect on the day, with three hits and a walk. Mike O'Keefe also had three hits and drove in a pair. The Friars now owned a 21-3 overall record. This latest victory was their fifteenth in a row, establishing a new school record. The previous high of fourteen was set in 1995.

BACK TO EARTH

Following a day off, the University of Hartford came in and did something that no team had been able to do for more than three weeks against the surging Friars; beat them. It took a lot of runs to do it. Providence's fourteen runs on seventeen hits were not enough to secure a victory and extend their winning streak. After eight innings, PC actually held a 13-10 lead, but errors and bases on balls opened the door to a huge 9th inning for the Hawks. They scored eight times, eventually coming away with an 18-14 victory of the Friars.

With the schedule about to take a difficult and crucial turn with a spate of Big East matchups, the Friars couldn't afford to play sloppy baseball and give games away. The real season was about the start. This was when it counted. Despite the home loss to Hartford, the team remained confident as they welcomed in West Virginia the very next day for a double dip.

Providence's woes continued, however, when a strong West Virginia team took both games of the double header. In the first game, Josh Burnham got knocked around, surrendering all twelve runs, eight of them coming in the first inning, and suffering his first loss of the season as the Friars fell 12-7. Neal McCarthy drove in five of the runs for Providence with a grand slam and a solo shot, but it wasn't nearly enough. In order to preserve the arms in the bullpen, Keith Reed was sent in to pitch and he threw two perfect innings.

In the second game, starting pitcher Rob Corraro also took his first loss of the season, going the distance in the 6-3 defeat. Neal McCarthy had another homerun in a losing cause.

Providence was now in the midst of a three-game losing streak, with a second doubleheader in as many days with another Big East rival, the University of Pittsburgh. In the first game, Marc DesRoches was called on to stop the bleeding, and the big right-hander delivered. After Pitt capitalized on a couple of errors, plating an unearned run in the 4th, and Marc served up a gopher ball in the 5th, the Friars were down 2-1. But Providence rallied in the 6th, scoring four runs after making two quick outs in the inning and defeated the Panthers 5-3. Marc improved his record to 5-1.

The second game was all Pittsburgh. They mashed their way to an 18-4 win, slugging eleven extra base hits, three of them leaving Hendricken Field.

A TOUGH STRETCH

There was no relief in sight with the upcoming schedule taking the Friars on the road for almost the entire month of April against conference rivals. They began the stretch with a couple of non-conference games, the first on March 29 at Holy Cross. The Friars got back on the winning track, cruising to a 12-4 win over the Crusaders. Stewy, in his longest outing of the season, 6.1 innings, earned his second win of the season. The Friars were out-hit, but they took advantage of several errors and got some timely hitting.

Back at Hendricken Field on March 30, Providence posted a 21-10 victory over the C.W. Post Pioneers of Long Island University. Freshman Ryan Lewis notched his fourth victory of the season against only one loss. But the Friar offense was the strength this day. They tallied twenty-one hits, ten of them for extra bases. Angelo had a big day, going 4-4 with a homerun, scoring five times and knocking in four. Paul Costello had a homer and four RBI. Keith Reed hit his team-leading ninth long ball of the season. Coley O'Donnell also struck one for the Friars when he came in to play first base in the 6th inning.

It was the fourth time that this Friar team recorded a hit total of twenty or more in a single game.

April began on a sour note when the team traveled to Indiana for two big games against Notre Dame but came up just short both times, losing 5-4 and 6-5. Josh Burnham was the hard luck loser in game one, done in by a costly infield error that later scored on a walk-off hit in the bottom of the 7th. This, after Neal McCarthy tied the game with a clutch three-run homer in the top of the inning. Despite the loss, Neal's teammates began to call him "Clutch" because of his knack of coming through in big situations with a game-tying or game-winning hit. They began to expect it from him.

Neal's round-tripper was only the third hit of the game for the Friars, their lowest hit total all season. On the hill for the Irish was the 6-5 right-hander, and future Major League pitcher, Aaron Heilman.

In between games, the Friars ate a prepared lunch in the stands while the Notre Dame players went into their clubhouse, undoubtedly for a catered meal. When they came out forty-five minutes later, they all had on new, clean uniforms and matching batting gloves. Everyone on the Providence side of the field noticed, and it only served to reinforce a "dirt dog" mentality that not only were they better than their opponents, but they were tougher. They didn't care about any of those fancy things that some of the other programs had. The only thing they cared about was playing hard all the time and winning.

In game two, Providence was bested once again on walk-off base hit, this time after Scooter singled home the game tying run in the top of the 9th. Rob Corraro went the distance in the Friars' 6-5 loss. They knew it was a game they could have won, leaving too many men on base.

As frustrating a day as it was for the entire team, Dan Conway probably had the worst day of anyone, and not just because he was 0-7 on the day. It was behind the plate that was the real problem. There was a promotion going at Eck Stadium that afternoon, with a local bakery giving away free bagels to a section of fans every time a Notre Dame player stole a base. So not only was the other team getting on base and running a lot, but Dan, who had a strong arm, couldn't throw anybody out. It wasn't all his fault. The Irish had a quick team, who got good jumps and picked good pitches to run on. To make matters worse, there was a guy in the stands behind the plate and every time someone would get on base he would start screaming, "Free bagels! Free bagels here! Love those bagels!" That went on every inning of both games. I was brutal for Dan. The rest of the team had a better time with it. In fact, they would rib their catcher about it for the rest of year, leaving bagels in his locker and in his catcher's bag, and anywhere else they could plant one. That afternoon, however, no one said a word to him, not even Coach Hickey.

CHAPTER 11   ROAD WARRIORS

DOWN TIME

After the two crushing defeats in Indiana, there was a bit of a break in the schedule. Providence had four days to prepare for their next game at Hendricken Field, a non-conference doubleheader against the University of Connecticut. With a team that had no tomorrow, staring at an entire weekend without games, the players focused on the present. They would be heading back to Providence the following morning, staying overnight at a hotel in South Bend, so the drinking began immediately after the second game. It was a way to unwind, and the team usually responded well to any amount of time off. They were in the midst of their toughest stretch in the schedule all year, and it was only going to get tougher with a lot of away games against some very good teams. The players knew what lay ahead and they needed to blow off some steam.

Several of the Friar faithful made the trip to Indiana with the team, including Plumber. Providence's Associate Athletic Director, Jerry Alaimo, had also come down. They were in the hotel bar with the coaches after dinner, but Coach Hickey and his staff did not stay long. When they went back to their rooms, the understanding was that the players were not permitted inside. However, not ten seconds after they walked out, the place was full of baseball players.

Normally, the team would have to abide by strict curfews and other rules of conduct regarding off-the-field behavior, including drinking, particularly on the road. This year however, the coaching staff was considerably lax on much of these rules.

In Providence, because the coaches also liked to unwind at Bradley Cafe, an unspoken agreement had been worked out with the players in which they would stay out of Brad's until the coaches left, which was typically by 9 p.m. It worked out perfectly, because the other students didn't go out until after 10 o'clock.

When Monday, April 5, came around, the Friars were ready. Whatever they did, it worked. They took care of business in a big way, taking two from the Huskies as the offense kicked into overdrive. They won the first game by a score of 14-2. Angelo had four hits and five RBI, slugging his sixth homerun of the season. Mike O'Keefe and Jamie Athas also went deep, and Marc DesRoches recorded his sixth win of the season.

In the game-two victory, three Friar pitchers got roughed up, allowing 18 runs, but the offense bailed them out by scoring twenty-five in an absolute slugfest. Numerous Big East single-game records fell that day, including most hits by a team (30, Providence), most hits by two teams (50), most runs scored by two team (43), most runs scored by a player (6, Scooter), most total bases by two teams (83), most at-bats by a player (7; Scooter and Paul Costello and Keith Reed).

Providence launched six homeruns in the game. Two of Dan Conway's five hits left the yard in the second game. Keith and Scooter both had a homerun and five hits. Neal McCarthy also homered, as did Mike O'Keefe, giving the Friars a total of nine homeruns in the doubleheader.

OFFENSIVE DISPLAY

Providence had 15 games remaining in the month of April, and all but one of them would be played on the road. On April 7, Boston College was the first stop, and while the Friar offense was up to the task, producing three homers and 11 runs, it wasn't enough. The pitching faltered, allowing 16 runs and serving up 6 homerun balls to the Eagles.

Putting the loss behind them, the following day the Friars visited the University of Rhode Island and beat up on the Rams 22-8. Ryan Lewis managed to get the win, despite giving up eight runs over six innings. He gave up four long balls, but the Friars provided him with and incredible nine homers of their own that afternoon. Keith Reed had a pair, but Freshman Jamie Athas had himself a day, connecting three times, good for 8 RBI.

The Friars next visited Washington, DC for a three games series against Georgetown, beginning with a doubleheader on

April 10. Providence won the first game 8-2 behind Marc DesRoches, who improved his record to 7-1 on the season. No homeruns were hit, but Scooter drove in four with a pair of hits. Providence took game two from the Hoyas by a score of 6-2. Josh Burnham won for the first time in nearly three weeks with a dominating performance, tossing a complete game five hitter and allowing only two unearned runs. Keith slugged homerun number fifteen on the season, Angelo his eighth.

The two teams met for a third game on April 12, and it was another decisive victory for Providence, 8-1. Rob Corraro made it look easy, tossing a complete game while Jeremy and Keith went yard.

Keith Reed was named Big East Player of Week and Scooter shared Rookie Of The Week honors.

The Friars returned to Hendricken Field on April 14 and avenged their loss to Boston College the week prior. Providence was trailing 8-4 entering the bottom of the 8th inning, but rallied for four runs, capped off by game-tying single off the bat of Jamie Athas. The game went to the home half of the 10th with the score still tied, when Jamie once again delivered a big hit, this one driving in Angelo, who had walked and advanced to second on a wild pitch, with the winning run. It was Jamie's third hit and third ribbie of the game, and he not-so-quietly extended his hitting streak to nine games while raising his overall season average to .342. Keith Reed homered in his third straight game, his seventeenth on the season. Paul Costello also went deep for the Friars and Marc DesRoches got credit for the win, his eighth, working the last 1.2 innings.

Harvard came in the following day and beat up on the Friars, scoring a lot of runs early against Ryan Lewis and winning the game 13-6. The Friars gave this one away, committing four costly errors and allowing eight unearned runs to score. Dan Conway hit a three-run shot and Angelo clouted his tenth homerun of the season in the loss.

The Friars were in South Orange, New Jersey on April 17 for a weekend series with Seton Hall. The teams split the twin bill, with Providence winning the opener behind Marc's 2-hit shutout. In the 2-0 victory, the Friars had only four singles themselves, getting three of them in the first inning and scoring two runs, but that was all they needed. It was Marc's ninth win of the year and his third in just seven days. It was the fourth time he won a game following a Friar loss, becoming the stopper for Providence. But Providence dropped the second game 11-3, letting the game get away in the 8th when the Pirates exploded for seven runs against Rob Corraro and Mike Stewart. The two teams met again the next day, with the Friars coming out on top, 10-8. Scooter had a huge day, collecting five hits, including his ninth triple of the season and Neal McCarthy drove in four.

Marc was named co-Pitcher Of The Week in the Big East for the week ending April 19, and Scooter, once again, received Rookie Of The Week distinction.

TAKING ONE FOR THE TEAM

On April 20, the Friars only had to travel to the other side of the city to play Brown University. Ryan Lewis started for Providence and struggled early on. In the first inning, he gave up two quick runs and was getting hit pretty hard, so Scott Swanjord was asked to get loose. Stork, who was scheduled to pitch the next day, got up and went down with Swanny just to protect him while he was warming up. The bullpen was down the right field line, just outside the field of play, a very dangerous spot. Ryan settled down and got out of the inning, but Swanny and Stork stayed down there in case Ryan got into any further trouble.

The next inning, the Friars came up and went down in order, but Scooter, after rolling over a pitch and hitting a weak grounder to second for the final out, was so upset with himself that he took his anger out onto the field with him. He was playing left, and between innings he was tossing the ball back and forth with Keith in center. His last AB was obviously still bothering him as he pounded the ball into Keith's glove. When the umpires called for the balls to be thrown in, he was supposed to throw his all the way across the outfield to the player who was warming up the right fielder. He gave it a little extra, however, and the ball sailed into the bullpen area where Swanny, Stork and backup catcher, Chris Caprio, were talking and not watching the ball.

Someone yelled, "Heads up!" And that's just what they did. They all looked up, including Stork, who was struck square in the mouth. One tooth got knocked out, another one was chipped and a third was loosened.

Swanny saw the tooth go flying out of Stork's mouth and he immediately got down on the ground and began scouring the grass for the incisor. He found both the whole tooth and the chipped piece, and picked them up. He gave them to Alan Segee, the trainer, who took Stork and his teeth to a local dentist. By the time they get to the office, the loose tooth had fallen out as well.

Back on the field, Ryan Lewis ended up going the distance and picked up his sixth win of the season as the Friars prevailed, 11-5. Scooter felt awful, and went to visit Stork after the game to offer his apologies.

The following day, the team traveled to Boston College and Stork took the ball, making his scheduled start. With swollen lips and a hole in his smile, he earned his fourth win of the season. Scooter, who had been wishing there was something he could do to make it up to Stork, found a way when hit for the cycle and drove in five runs in the Friars 8-3 victory. The left-handed leadoff hitter for the Friars started the game by cracking a double, hit a three-run homer in the second inning, singled in the fourth and then tripled in two runs in the top of the ninth.

STRETCH RUN

There were a couple days before the start of a big three-game weekend series in New Brunswick, New Jersey, and as usual, the boys partied hard but were ready to play on Saturday, April 24 against a very talented Rutgers team. They split a double header that day, winning the first game 9-6 behind Marc DesRoches, who earned his tenth win of the season against only one defeat. It wasn't his prettiest win, but he pitched all seven innings and struck out nine without walking a batter. The Friar offense provided him with fifteen hits, seven of them going for doubles. Scooter had three of the two-baggers himself. Angelo contributed four hits, including a homerun.

The Friars dropped a heartbreaker, 15-14, in the nightcap. Every pitcher who stepped onto the mound got hammered. Both clubs pounded out 17 hits. Paul Costello and Scooter had four apiece and Okie slugged the lone Friar homerun of the game, his tenth of the season.

After eight and a half innings, the Friars were clinging to a 14-13 lead. In the bottom of the 9th Stork got called into the game.

After retiring the first batter on a groundout to first, he walked the next batter, pinch-hitting in the #9 slot. The top of the order was up next, and David DeJesus, the future Major Leaguer, delivered a double, setting the Scarlet Knights up to steal the game from the Friars. And that was just what they did, as Stork's very next pitch was hit through the right side of the infield for a single, bringing home the tying run and DeJesus with the game winner just ahead of the throw from the outfield.

It was a devastating way to lose and Rutgers was a team Providence really wanted to beat. They already knew they could play with those guys, so their confidence was not shaken, despite the disappointing loss. The Friars proved it the next day as they slugged their way to an 11-4 victory over their conference rivals. Josh Burnham pitched a complete game and improved his record to 7-2. Providence's 19-hit attack was led by Mike O'Keefe, who had four hits, including another homerun and 4 RBI. Neal McCarthy had three hits, one a homerun, to go with 4 RBI. Keith Reed also had three hits for the Friars.

The game marked the end of the road schedule for the Friars in the regular season. The team was in great shape for the upcoming playoffs, carrying a 37-13 overall record and a respectable 12-8 in the Big East. They had eight games remaining, all against Big East teams and all at home. How well they did during this final homestand would determine their seeding in the Big East Tournament in the middle of May.

Before the next series with St. John's, the Friars had a full week off for final exams. With no baseball, that meant two things to this team; studying and partying. The extended time off, and everything they did between the April 25 win at Rutgers and the May 2 double dip against the Red Storm, hardly broke their stride as they took two games from St. John's, 9-1 and 12-9.

Marc set a new school mark by winning his eleventh game of the season. Todd Incantalupo won ten, the previous Friar high, which he did twice, in 1995 and 1996. Incantalupo was drafted and went on to play in the Milwaukee Brewers organization. Marc pitched all seven innings, allowing five hits and striking out seven. Jamie Athas slugged a two-run homer and Neal McCarthy and Keith Reed had three hits for the Friars.

In the nightcap, St. John's put some late inning runs on the board to chase Rob Corraro from the game, but the Friars held on, taking advantage of nine free passes. Scooter had three hits and scored four times. Neal McCarthy hit his twelfth homerun and Okie drove in three.

THE GUY ACROSS THE STREET

There was a lot of excitement on that two-win afternoon, and not just on the field. With the weather warming up, and the games at Providence dwindling down to a precious few, there were many more PC fans in attendance than normal. But there were also some people in the neighborhood who were actually happy to see baseball disappear from the college, though perhaps none more than The Guy Across The Street.

River Avenue runs directly along the first base line, the row of ranch and two-story family residences on the other side of the street separated from the field by a chain link fence and a narrow stand of trees. Needless to say, foul balls were constantly landing on River Avenue, occasionally striking and denting passing cars. Home plate was no more than a hundred feet from the front door of the nearest house, and several were in the direct line of fire. The Guy Across The Street may not have been the recipient of more unwanted baseballs on his lawn than his neighbors, but he was the most vocal. He had an aluminum awning over his front door that attracted baseballs like a magnet. This afternoon one foul ball too many found his awning.

As usual, one of the freshman players would jog across the street to retrieve the balls that left the playing field. The Guy Across The Street would sometimes already have it in his possession and the player would head back to the dugout empty-handed. He had never given a ball back that he got to first. This time, however, he walked across the street with the ball in one hand and a baseball bat in the other. He made his way to the fence behind the plate and started yelling about the dents to his awning and how sick and tired he was of it happening. He demanded compensation for a new awning and wanted to know who was in charge.

The Guy Across The Street was told that he needed to get in touch with senior assistant Athletic Director, Jerry Alaimo, and he immediately scoffed upon hearing this.

"Alaimo?" he shouted. "You mean, A-*lame*-o. That guy was a lousy basketball player, a lousy coach (Alaimo was a former basketball coach at Brown University) and he's a lousy A.D."

He made other derogatory remarks about the college, the baseball program and anything else that he could think of. When he finished his rant, Tim Connors, the Sports Information Director, sidled up beside him and asked for his phone number so that it could be passed on to Jerry, which he begrudgingly gave. However, at the same time that Tim was writing it down, several others who were standing nearby overheard the conversation and one of them took the number down also. The Guy Across the Street then turned and stormed off, walking back home and carrying the ball and his bat with him like a kid in sandlot.

Late that same night, The Guy Across the Street received a phone call from someone who said he was Jerry Alaimo (it was not) and demanded that all the baseballs he confiscated through the years be returned to the school, pronto. The Guy Across the Street, naturally, started screaming so loud that he could not hear the uproarious laughter in the background on the other end of the phone.

It was a childish prank, for sure, but a harmless one, and much too amusing for the guys making the calls to stop after that night.

The next day, Providence beat St. John's again. Josh Burnham, despite allowing three homeruns, pitched the Friars to a complete game 11-7 victory and a three-game series sweep. Scooter and Angelo went back to back in the 1st inning for the home team and Neal McCarthy drove in three runs, pacing the Friar's 13-hit attack.

The victory clinched a Big East Tournament berth for the Friars, but that was really just the beginning of what this team wanted to accomplish.

The game also featured another personal appearance from The Guy Across the Street. He stalked along the chain link fence around the field like a caged animal, demanding to know who had called him so late the previous night. He departed with only stares and sniggers, threatening to call the police. For weeks afterward, he would be taunted by phone calls from people who altered their voices and repeatedly said, "We want the balls back," and then hung up.

Marc DesRoches was named Big East Pitcher Of The Week for the second time in three weeks. Down the stretch, PC's ace was hitting his stride. It was a good sign for the Friars heading into the conference playoffs. That same week, Scooter was named Big East Rookie Of The Week for the third straight week, and the fourth time in five weeks.

CHAPTER 12   LAST HURRAH

TAKING TWO

There was another big layoff before the next and final series of games at Hendricken Field. It was graduation weekend at Providence College, but for twenty-five Friars there was something even more important taking place on school grounds at that time.

The players all felt a mix of excitement and sadness leading up to the dates with Villanova. Not playing for ten days only gave them more time to think about it.

Coach Hickey knew that his players were amped up, wanting nothing more than to win all three games that final weekend. He didn't need to give any rah-rah speeches to motivate them, and he didn't want to temper their enthusiasm in any way. He wanted them to remain focused on the larger goal, but he also wanted them to enjoy what was happening and not put too much pressure on themselves. Going all out and having nothing left in the tank for the upcoming Big East Tournament would not help their cause. He would stress that these three games would not affect their playoff chances. They were already in, which meant they would be playing at least two more games in the tournament the following week regardless of what they did against Villanova.

"We have five more chances," Coach Hickey told his players, "not three, to be part of something that we're never going to forget. Let's win as many games as we can and let's not take anything for granted."

It was one of the few times all year that he ever made any reference about the season being the last for baseball at Providence.

The double-header on Friday afternoon began with Marc DesRoches trying for an unprecedented twelfth win of the season for a Friar starter. Providence came out of the gate swinging. Scooter started things off for the Friars with a leadoff double.

After Angelo got hit by a pitch and Keith Reed walked, the bases were loaded for Neal McCarthy. The freshman right fielder whom his teammates called "Clutch," cracked a grand slam that put Providence on top, 4-0. It was his lucky thirteenth homerun of the season. It was all the scoring that the Friars would get in the game, but it was also all they would need. Marc pitched all seven innings, limiting Villanova to three runs on four hits while striking out nine. With the victory, Marc ended the regular season with an overall record of 12-1 to go with a superb 2.44 ERA.

It was a truly incredible season for the fifth-year senior right-hander, but it was far from over.

The second game of the day was even closer, requiring an extra frame to decide. The Friars hurt themselves with three early errors that led to three runs, but PC was still up 8-5 when Rob Corraro took his team into the 8th inning. After striking out the first batter of the inning on three pitches, he walked the Wildcats leadoff hitter and was pulled for lefty Andy Scott. Stork hit the first batter he faced and then gave up a long homerun to the #3 hitter and just like that the ballgame was knotted at eight. Stork settled down and got the final two outs and then worked two more scoreless innings. In the 10th the Friars won the game in an anticlimactic fashion when four consecutive walks forced in the game-winning run, Jamie Athas scoring on the free pass to Paul Costello. The 400 spectators stood and cheered wildly as if it had been a walk-off homerun.

THE FINAL GAME

Going into the finale at Hendricken Field the following day, May 15, the team was enjoying a successful season, rated best in the Northeast and 26th in the nation in a poll of coaches. They owned a 42-13 record, two victories short of the school total season record. Outwardly, the Friars were only looking to close out the season with a seven-game winning streak and momentum going into the Big East Tournament, but the reality was that they were playing for much more than that. It was not just the final game of the season, it was the last baseball game that was ever going to be played at Providence College.

1,200 fans and supporters turned out to witness the historic game. Providence College president, Father Philip A. Smith was not among them.

Commencement exercises were taking place the next day, and Smith said he was busy with speaking engagements the entire day and he "didn't have a minute's time for anything else."

Rev. Terence J. Keegan, the school's executive vice president and designated spokesman, revealed something more telling when he said, "He (Father Smith) was advised that it might be a hostile environment. And we wanted this day and this team not to be mired in ugliness, but to go out in a blaze of glory. They deserve that."

Weather conditions could not have been more perfect; Sunny, 70-degrees and just enough puffy white clouds to break up the high blue sky. The infield dirt had been raked and watered by PC players. Fresh white chalk had been applied to the baselines. The metal bleachers along the fences were chock-full. Lawn chairs had been set up behind the backstop and blankets laid out on the grass beyond the outfield wall. Hendricken Field and the surrounding campus of Providence College had a carnival atmosphere to it; everyone was waiting for something to cheer about.

The media coverage was unprecedented for a PC baseball game. Regional radio sports talk station, 99.7 The Score, was broadcasting the game live. Radio personality, Scott Cordischi, was interviewing the crowd and would be doing the play-by-play for his listeners.

Before the start of the game, each player and coach was introduced on the crackling p.a. system, their individual contributions briefly noted by announcer, John Dolan. The fans stood and applauded for each one. Lou Merloni, Big East co-Player Of The Year in 1993 for the Friars, wanted to be involved in the pre-game ceremonies. He caught two ceremonial first pitches tossed by two former Friar head coaches, Alex Nahigian, who was at the helm from 1960-1978, and Don Mezzanotte, who took the reins from 1979-1989.

"I give these kids all the respect and credit in the world," Merloni said afterward. "All that they've gone through this year, they could have quit on themselves they way the school quit on them, but they didn't. They're going out on top."

And then it was time to play the game. On the hill for Providence was Josh Burnham. At high noon, he delivered the first pitch. A low fastball split the plate in half and was swung on and missed by the leadoff hitter. The crowd reacted. That set the tone for the early part of the game in which pitching dominated. Villanova got on the board first with a solo homer in the 4th inning, but the Friars quickly tied the score in the bottom of the inning. They gave up the lead in the 5th, falling behind 2-1, but they came right back again, this time with two of their own, highlighted by a run-scoring triple by Scooter, who scampered home with go-ahead run on a ground out by Paul Costello. Providence never looked back, scoring a run in the 6th, another in the 7th and two more in the 8th. They built a 7-2 lead entering the 9th. When Villanova scored two and threatened for more, with two on and one out and the top of the Wildcats order coming up, Josh remained in the game. The fans were on edge, quiet with expectation. The senior right-hander then delivered his 133rd pitch of the afternoon. When Villanova's Pat King hit a high chopper to third, everyone held their breath. Angelo fielded the ball and went to second to start a double play. Paul Costello received the ball to get the runner at second and then pivoted to make the relay throw to first, getting the ball to Okie just ahead of the runner. As soon as the umpire made the "out" call at first base, the large crowd of family, friends and students streamed onto the field to celebrate with the players, who congratulated and hugged one another, many with tears in their eyes.

Postgame festivities began with the players making curtain calls and acknowledging the fans, who went crazy as John Dolan called their names one by one over the p.a. Afterward, sports talk radio host Scott Cordischi interviewed the coaches and the players. Other local and national media outlets converged on the Friars for comments.

"I love it here," Scooter told one reporter. With his two hits that afternoon, he was leading the nation with 105. "I love the school. I love the guys. We're a family. I wish I didn't have to leave."

Coach Charlie Hickey was milling around the field, congratulating his players, receiving as many accolades as he gave out. The win that day was significant to him on an individual level, as it marked his 100th victory as the Friars head coach. "This was a special day," he acknowledged. "This will be a year that none of us will ever forget." He added, remarking about Title IX, "It wasn't meant to have this kind of negative impact. We all want fairness. There just has to be another way."

For Josh Burnham, he won for the ninth time that season against only two losses, and incredibly it was his eighth complete game. He also went over the 100-inning mark for the season, the first time any pitcher had done that in school history. Angelo led the Friar offense by driving in three runs with three hits, including a homerun in the 6th inning, the last ever at Hendricken Field in Providence. It was an honor for both seniors to be a Friar and to be part of the history of Providence College baseball.

A keg outside the fence in left field had been tapped. Players stayed on the field with family and friends and alumni, talking, taking pictures, embracing. They did not want to leave. They knew they would not be coming back. Then, as the sun began to drop behind the trees there were fewer voices as one by one people began to drift away from Hendricken Field. Eighty years after the sport originated at Providence College, it was also disappearing. It was really happening. In fact, it already had. A field of dreams was coming to end, but there was still a little bit of magic left in this Friars squad.

STEPPING TO THE PLATE

The school was not about to do anything for the baseball team, so Plumber and Brian Feeny stepped to plate and organized a steak fry for the players that night after the game at their own expense.

The administration had been approached weeks before, during the planning stage, and asked about providing a hall or outdoor location for the event. However, they would not grant permission to have the cookout take place anywhere on campus, giving no official reason. They seemed to have already washed their hands of the whole program. But that did not deter these guys. Because of the numbers of people expected, Bradley Cafe was too small to accommodate everyone comfortably, so they rented the VFW Post Hall a few blocks away on Veazie Street. A band was hired to play and some tickets were sold beforehand to offset some of the upfront cost.

A large crowd quickly gathered, even more than had been anticipated. There was plenty of beer and food. It was a party atmosphere, for sure, with current students and alumni coming together to celebrate the success of the Providence baseball program and also to mourn the end of the national pastime and a neighborhood tradition.

When a majority of this crowd dissipated, it was back to Brad's. The players were drinking and reminiscing, and the more they drank the angrier some of them became. Finally, enough beer had been consumed that it occurred to a couple of the players that they should take a little something back. Once the idea was floated out there to remove home plate from Hendricken Field, capture it like a flag in a war game, they acted on it immediately. Led by Jarrod Brucato, an injured senior walk-on who sat out the year, a small group of players took their beers with them and a couple of shovels and walked the quarter mile to the field. After hopping the perimeter fence, they gathered around home plate and finished their beers, as if in a final tribute. Then they unceremoniously ripped the plate out of the ground, much the way that some of the players felt school administrators had ripped the hearts out of their chests. They were surprised at how easily it came out. More than a symbol of the game that would never again be played on the grounds of Providence College, it was a piece of history, and these players, who were barely twenty-one years old, understood this implicitly. The plate had registered countless runs, along with game-winning runs that produced jubilant pig pile celebrations for Friar teams of the past. So many future pro players stood on either side of that plate through the years, including Mo Vaughn when he was playing for Seton Hall. Big Mo may always be most remembered for hitting perhaps the longest homerun in the history of Hendricken Field, purportedly driving one off Hopkins Hall in deep centerfield. It was the same plate that Coach Hickey had them all gather around that dark day in October when he broke the news to them that their sport had been cut.

The plate was secreted back to Bradley Café and placed on the bar between the remaining players, who toasted to everything that it represented. They stayed there all night, but eventually they had to go home. The plate, however, never left, and today it remains at Bradley Cafe, permanently preserved in a glass frame (courtesy of Plumber) mounted on the wall and signed by all the 1999 team members, as well as others former players who had come through Brad's over the past ten years.

There were other pieces of equipment and baseball-related items that had been pilfered later on, some of it donated to other school programs that could make use of it, including the infield tarpaulin, which ended being gifted anonymously to the Bryant College baseball program in nearby Smithfield.

After Brad's closed that night, an even smaller group continued the party at the Baseball House, where it started to get loud and rowdy enough for a neighbor to complain and call the police. Realizing who was knocking on the door at such a late hour, the players became nervous. Everyone panicked, running all around. Plumber, however, sat calmly and continued drinking. Someone opened the door and a cop came inside.

"Screw," Plumber told the officer. "Get out here. Leave us alone, you prick."

The players were stunned, amazed by the way Plumber was talking to the cop, who just smiled and laughed. They found out later it was Plumber's brother.

1999 Big East Conference – Regular Season Final Standings

	Big East Record	Overall Record
Notre Dame	20-5	41-14
Rutgers	19-7	35-17
PROVIDENCE	**18-8**	**43-13**
Seton Hall	14-11	31-17-1
St. John's	13-11-1	29-20-2
West Virginia	12-13	29-26
Villanova	11-15	27-26-1
Pittsburgh	11-15	27-27
Boston College	10-15-1	26-21-1
Connecticut	10-16	27-24
Georgetown	2-24	18-34

CHAPTER 13   BIG EAST TOURNAMENT

UNFINISHED BUSINESS

Sunday, May 16 was graduation day at Providence College. Nine seniors on the baseball team received their diplomas that day, including Josh Burnham, Chris Caprio, Angelo Ciminiello, Rob Corraro, Josh Cox, Paul Costello, Marc DesRoches, Todd Murray and Scott Swanjord.

However, these nine players, and the other members of the 1999 Providence College baseball team were not going anywhere just yet. They had some unfinished business to take care of.

Over the course of the last three months, numerous single-season team and individual records had been established. The Friars, who had been picked to finished seventh in their conference, had been ranked #1 among New England teams all season long. Their 18 conference wins was a school high and their 43 wins was a regular season best, surpassing by one the total by the 1995 Friar team.

They made their point to the administration, but this was a determined bunch that was focused on a bigger prize, the first step of which was the Big East Tournament.

The 1999 Big East Conference Baseball Championship was a four-day, double-elimination tournament to be played in Mercer County Waterfront Park, in Trenton, New Jersey. It was the home of the Trenton Thunder, the Double-A affiliate of the Boston Red Sox. One of the conference's top six teams would emerge victorious and earn a berth into the 1999 NCAA Division I Baseball Championships.

The six teams included the top-seeded Fighting Irish of Notre Dame, the defending 1998 champs Rutgers next, followed by Providence, then Seton Hall, St. John's and West Virginia.

For post-season play, the Friar players were given new undershirts. They were also black, with the PC baseball logo and the words, "WE JUST WANT IT MORE."

AWARDS SWEEP

On May 18, the day before the scheduled start of the Tournament, the annual Big East Banquet was held at Waterfront Park facilities and Providence swept the ceremonies, garnering all four major awards.

Keith Reed received Big East Player Of The Year honors, joining Roger Haggerty, 1986, Lou Merloni, 1993 and Bob O'Toole, 1995, as the only Friars to win the award. Keith hit 17 homers in 1999 regular season, and 36 for his career, which tied a school record, shared with Ed Walsh. His 68 RBI heading into the Tournament was already a Friar single-season record.

Marc DesRoches was named the Big East Pitcher Of The Year, compiling a 12-1 overall record, including 8-0 with one save in Big East competition to go with a league-best 2.61 ERA. Only two other Friar hurlers could boast such an honor, Jim Navilliat, 1986 and Mike Macone, 1995.

Big East Rookie Of The Year was none other than Providence's standout leadoff hitter, Mike Scott. Scooter finished the regular season with a .429 batting average. The national hit-leader also struck a nation-leading total of 12 triples, including eight in Big East play, a new conference record. Lou Merloni, 1990 and Todd Incantalupo, 1995, were the other PC rookies to receive this award. Scooter was named singularly or shared honors for Big East Rookie Of The Week five times during the course of the season. He also tied Okie for the most doubles (21) on the team.

Head Coach Charlie Hickey was named Big East Coach Of The Year for guiding PC to what was arguably their most successful season in school history. The popular coach, completing his third year as skipper, owned a 100-58-1 record heading into the 1999 Big East Tournament.

In the history of the ceremonies, no other Big East team has won all four awards.

NO TOMORROW

Heavy rain on Wednesday washed out Providence's first-round game with Seton Hall. That day, the Tournament's opening game between Notre Dame and West Virginia was in the bottom of the seventh inning, with the Fighting Irish leading 3-0 and threatening for more, when the skies opened up. After a five hour delay, the game was called. It would continue where it left off the following day, but the delay pushed the championship round of the double-elimination tournament from Saturday to Sunday.

So on Thursday night, May 20, the Friars took on fourth-seeded Seton Hall, a team who they played three times during the regular season, winning two of the games. The game one matchup was touted to be a classic pitcher's duel between two All-Big East selections, the Friars' Marc DesRoches and Seton Hall's Cameron Esslinger. Instead, it turned out to be a slugfest, reminding everyone that if baseball is anything, it is unpredictable. Esslinger, who had been drafted by the Milwaukee Brewers the previous year, didn't make it out of the third inning, and Marc, the Big East Pitcher of the Year, struggled throughout his 6.2 innings, allowing nine runs, six earned and four homers.

The Friar offense, however, picked up the big right-hander, who had given them so much throughout the season. Both teams exchanged a run in the 1st inning, but then Providence scored twice in the 2nd and six times in the 3rd powered by a three-run bomb by Dan Conway. Providence took a 9-1 lead into the 5th as Marc seemed to be cruising along. Then the Pirates brought out the big bats, scoring eight runs with four homers over the next three innings. A solo shot by Neal McCarthy in the 6th proved to be the decisive run and Stork came in to relieve Marc in the 7th, tossing 2.1 innings of shutout baseball to preserve the 10-9 lead and hand Marc his thirteenth win of the season.

The six homeruns in the game tied a single-game Tournament record and brought the first-round total to a whopping thirteen in just three games, more homeruns than had been hit in the entire Tournament the year before (12), which became the new tournament high at the time. With record crowds turning out, and the Friars notching their 44th win of the season, tying the school-best mark, Providence seemed to be a team of destiny.

The following day, however, Providence suffered its first loss of the tournament, an 11-4 defeat at the hands of Rutgers

University, who also snapped the Friars' eight game winning streak. The Scarlet Knights pounded out eighteen hits, with every batter accounting for at least one, while the PC offense managed only three, all of them singles. Providence scratched out a couple of runs in the 1st inning to take an early 2-0 lead. Rutgers' sophomore lefty Brian Delehanty had trouble locating his pitches, walking two and hitting two batters, one with the bases loaded that plated Scooter with the first run of the ballgame. Angelo then singled in Paul Costello with the Friar's second unearned run.

After the rocky first inning, Delehanty settled down and let the Rutgers potent offense take over. Rutgers offense had been ranked in the top ten nationally in team batting average for much of the year, and finished the season with a .376 BA. Josh Burnham got tagged for ten runs on fifteen hits before being lifted in the sixth after giving up back to back jacks. The victory was Fred Hill's 500th in sixteen seasons as Rutgers' head coach.

For Josh, it was only his third loss of the season, and after the game he didn't know if he had pitched his last game as a Friar. Since this was a double-elimination tournament, the boys were not done, but the Providence College Friars baseball program was now just one loss away from becoming history. Facing the top-seeded and 25th nationally-ranked Fighting Irish of Notre Dame in the morning, things were not about to get any easier.

Providence had already dropped two to Notre Dame in a double-header loss earlier in the season, both close games. Going back to the 1998 Big East Tournament, the Friars had been eliminated by Notre Dame by a score of 9-7 in a semifinal game, though first baseman Mike O'Keefe had almost won it for his team when he hit a deep fly to right field in the 8th inning that missed going over the fence for a three-run homer by a few feet. The bitter loss to the Irish in the previous year's Tournament was not forgotten by Okie or the rest of the team.

Anyway you cut it, it was a must win for the Friars, with everything on the line. If there was ever a sense of urgency, it would have been now. But this team had been playing on borrowed time since they started practice in October and they remained determined to make the most of the opportunity they had left.

TEAM SPORT

The Notre Dame game was huge, but you might never have guessed it by the behavior of some of the Friar players. Going back to their hotel after their resounding loss to Rutgers, the players were markedly relaxed. They certainly knew what they were up against. They were long-shot underdogs in this one, but that was okay. They had been underestimated all season. They understood that in order to beat the squad that was going to be on the field against them the following day they would have to play their best ball. Notre Dame featured several Major League-caliber ballplayers, including pitcher Aaron Heilman. If PC's season did end with a loss to Notre Dame, the Friars would have nothing to be ashamed of. In fact, they could still be quite proud of their season and the run they had into the playoff tournament. But they were destined for bigger things, and maybe they knew it, tempting fate with a confidence and swagger befitting a team that had actually won something.

The focus remained baseball, and the partying was actually kept to a minimum, but there were distractions and temptations in the female form all around. The hotel was stupid with beautiful girls from all the Big East college campuses. It was difficult for anyone not to notice them. It was impossible for Todd Murray not to notice them. So it was not surprising when he met a co-ed from New Zealand and struck up a conversation with her. It wasn't even that big of a deal when Jeremy Sweet joined Todd and the young woman and they all disappeared behind a closed door later that night. However, it became somewhat of an international incident the next morning when the entire team was expected to meet for breakfast and, needless to say, Todd and Jeremy did not make it. As a consequence, Jeremy was pulled from the starting lineup by Coach Hickey. Jason Hairston was inserted into centerfield, Keith was shifted to right and Neal McCarthy would be the hitter.

Jason hadn't figured on seeing much action before the 8th inning, so he probably did the most drinking of any Friar the night before. When his number was called, however, he was ready to answer the bell.

In the end, the move proved not only to be the right one, but a difference-maker, as Providence went on to upset Notre Dame by a score of 8-4.

Rob Corraro went nine for his eighth win of the season and Providence pounded out fifteen hits in the game, paced by Jason Hairston, who was making his first start for the Friars since way back on April 20. Jason went 3-4 out of the nine-hole. He singled, doubled and tripled in five trips, and also laid down a sacrifice bunt. He scored a run and his triple in the top of the 9th with two men aboard extended Providence's lead to four. Scooter singled three times and drove in two, while Okie contributed a pair of hits and two RBIs.

Because the Fighting Irish had already been beaten by Seton Hall, the loss to Providence eliminated them from the Big East Tournament. However, while Notre Dame could not be crowned conference champions, they had already secured a berth in the NCAA Division I Tournament, having been afforded an automatic spot into the expanded 64-team field because they had been selected to host one of the 16 sub-regional tournaments. All host teams were guaranteed berths. This was the first year that a format of 16 four-team sub-regionals had been adapted, replacing the 8 six-team regionals playoff setup that they had been using in years past.

For Providence, the victory was number 45 on the year, making the 1999 farewell season the most winning in school history.

There was little time to savor the win because they had to face Rutgers for the second time in the Tournament that same night, with their backs remaining against the wall.

ONE STEP CLOSER

Stork's turn in the rotation came up, and he would be put to the test against Rutgers' highly vaunted offense, which had scored 38 runs in its three Tournament games, including the 11 they put on the board against the Friars the day before.

Stork did not forget how he had taken it on the chin a month earlier when he came in as a reliever and gave up the game-winning runs to the same Rutgers team in a 15-14 loss. He was looking to even the score this time around.

In the bottom of the 1st inning, Stork spotted the Scarlet Knights an early run when future Major Leaguer, David DeJesus, smacked a leadoff homerun on the second pitch thrown to him.

That remained the only run of the game until Providence came to bat in the 5th inning. Jason Hairston, once again playing centerfield and batting ninth, started things by reaching base on a one-out throwing error by third baseman, Jake Daubert. From the bench, Jeremy Sweet was screaming the loudest for Jason and all his Friar teammates. After two consecutive singles by Scooter and Paul Costello loaded the bases, Okie drew a walk that forced Jason home and tied the game at one apiece. Keith Reed came up next and hit the first pitch he saw on the ground to short. Okie was forced at second but Keith beat the relay throw to first, keeping the inning alive as Scooter scored the go ahead run. 2-1, Providence.

With two outs, Neal McCarthy stepped to the left side of the plate looking for something inside after having been pitched up-and-in his previous two at-bats. He was not fooled when Rutgers starter Eric Brown tried to sneak an inside changeup by him. The ball stayed up in the zone a little too long and Neal launched a towering three-run homer, his fifteenth of the year. The ball soared over the centerfield fence and splashed into the Delaware River. Just like that it was 5-1.

Stork was able to keep Rutgers off the board until the 7th, when the first two batters reached on successive singles. A potential big inning was averted when Providence turned a 4-6-3 double play because the next hitter struck a run-scoring single. Stork got out of further trouble by inducing a pop out to the catcher that ended the threat.

Despite allowing a dozen hits, Stork limited the damage to only two runs in a complete game, 136-pitch effort. The virtually unknown lefty, only two years removed from the obscurity of high school baseball, pitched the game of his life.

Providence tacked on four runs in the 9th and the Friars 9-2 victory set them up to play for the conference championship the following afternoon against the winner of the St. John's/Rutgers matchup.

For the Knights, it was their first loss in the tournament. The year before, when they won the whole thing, they had done it after overcoming an early loss, so they remained confident that they could still get it done, figuring they would end up playing Providence for a third time in the tournament, and for the championship, once they beat St. John's later that night. But it was not in the cards, as St. John's defeated Rutgers and set up a showdown against the Friars the following day, May 23, at high noon. The winner would be the 1999 Big East Champs.

Fifth-seeded St. John's was playing with a lot of momentum, winning three straight after losing their first-round game.

Coach Hickey had a few options, but a difficult choice to make. He could go with Ryan Lewis or Stewy in the championship game. He could piecemeal it, using several arms to try to get the job done. But he knew his best chance rested with his ace, Marc DesRoches. When he asked Marc to come see him, before the coach opened his mouth, the big right-hander said, "I want the ball."

"How do you feel, Marc?"

"I feel great."

That was good enough for Coach Hickey, despite Marc's rough outing last time out against Seton Hall, a game in which he had thrown 137 pitches, and despite the fact that he would be working on just two days rest, something he had never done before. Following elbow surgery in December, he had been pretty much limited to five days of rest between starts, but Coach Hickey knew in a game of this magnitude, you go out with your best.

BIG EAST CHAMPIONSHIP

Some of the Providence fans who traveled to New Jersey to support the Friars were staying in the same hotel as the players. They celebrated the team's wins that day and night along with the players. Some of the celebrants had indulged all night, and on the morning of the championship game they were up early, or still up from the night before. Among them was George Colli, the sophomore pitcher who sat out the season after surgery to remove a testicular lump. They were all perched in the lobby when the Notre Dame players were leaving the hotel to get on their bus for the trip back to Indiana. Some of the Friar faithful were still drinking, and as the team filed by in their suits and ties the Providence fans raised their drinks, in mock salute. Some were wearing PC shirts and hats, which others pointed to and cheered, "Go Providence! Go Providence!"

The Friar players were more subdued. This was the game they had been preparing for since last fall. 60 games, 46 wins and it all came down to these next 9 innings. Marc had his game face on as he was throwing his warm up pitches before the game. He was embarrassed by his performance in his previous start against Seton Hall and he was looking to atone for it in a big way that afternoon.

By midday it was 80 degrees, overcast with sunny breaks and a slight breeze blowing off the river from right to left field. When Marc took the mound to begin the game he did not feel nervous. He wanted to be perfect, and he nearly was. Like Providence's previous two games in which they won, they spotted the opposing team a lead in the 1st inning. A leadoff walk and two singles produced the first run of the game. But that would be all the damage that the Red Storm would do that afternoon. In the bottom of the 1st the Friars scored four times and they never looked back. Marc took control of the game from there, allowing just five more hits to go along with 8 K's over the final eight frames.

When the final out was made, a ground out to Jamie at short, the nine players on the field threw up their hands and converged on Marc near the pitcher's mound. The Friars who had been perched on the top step of the dugout leaped up and joined them, piling on top of one another as more than a hundred fans who had traveled from Providence cheered wildly from the stands directly behind the dugout. Some of them came down to join the celebration. The tears that were shed by Friars on the field that day were tears of joy.

The Providence College Friars were the 1999 Big East Conference Champions, the school's first conference title since 1992, and earned their ninth NCAA berth, the first since 1995. Their season was extended at least two more games as a result of the win, with a chance to go even further than anyone expected. The 6-1 victory gave Marc DesRoches his fourteenth win of the season, his thirteenth in a row, and he finished the season with 82 K's, both single-season PC records that will last forever.

The St. John's players watched the Friars celebrating on the field with a combination of disappointment and awe, as if they were witnessing destiny.

Red Storm head coach, Ed Blankmeyer said after, "Those kids were hungry. When we played them in Providence, you saw it in their eyes. In my heart, I didn't want to face them in this tournament because you weren't playing against just the men. You were playing against a bunch of kids with heart."

St. John's catcher, Rob Fierro, added, "There's no next year for them. When you get all guys playing for a common goal, they're tough to beat. And it showed."

While the success of the 1999 Friars season had been a team effort in which every player contributed, quite possibly the Tournament win might not have been if Jeremy Sweet had not been taken out of the lineup and replaced by Jason Hairston just before the matchup with Notre Dame. Not only did Jason's 3 for 4 help Providence upset the heavily favored Fighting Irish, but Coach Hickey, going with the hot bat, left Jason in the lineup for the rest of the Tournament and he wound up leading the team with a .500 BA. In an alternate history where Jeremy Sweet made breakfast and happened to not play well that day, an 0-for-4 could have resulted in a loss to Notre Dame, with PC being eliminated from the tournament right then and there.

It's just another example of the unpredictability of baseball.

LOOKING AHEAD

A short time after the conclusion of the game, during the awards presentation ceremony, Marc and Angelo were called to home plate to accept the trophy signifying that the Providence College Friars were the 1999 Big East Conference Champions. The two team captains, however, would not go alone. They insisted that the entire team walk out with them so that the championship trophy could be presented to all 25 members whose combined efforts went into making their championship dream a reality. The players were all smiles as they hugged and congratulated one another for this proud achievement.

Marc was named The Most Outstanding Player of the Tournament, throwing 15.2 innings and posting a 4.02 ERA with two victories and no defeats. But it was his courageous effort in the championship game, going on short rest, that stacked the voting in his favor, and deservedly so.

Next up for the Big East champs was a first-round matchup in the NCAA Division I regional playoffs against Jacksonville on May 28 at Tallahassee, Florida's Dick Howser Stadium. The double-elimination tournament paired Providence against the #2 nationally-ranked host team Florida State University in the second round. The Citadel Bulldogs was the other team in the Tallahassee Regional Playoff series.

In the 80-year history of Providence College baseball, the Friars had never played any of these teams before. In their eight previous visits to the NCAA's, Providence owned a 5-17 record, but this year's team was looking to better that mark.

The Friars, of course, entered the 64-team national tournament as a dark horse, but now they were Big East Champions, and no one could doubt them anymore.

HOMECOMING

When the Friars returned home to Providence, fans and the players' family members awaited their arrival, rallying around the team and encouraging them to go as far as they could. There was a lot of pride to go around. The team felt it and the fans expressed it, but from Father Smith and the school administration, the team did not receive any sort of acknowledgement whatsoever. In fact, it was thought that they were privately unhappy with the team's advancement, if only because the school would have to foot the bill for their travel expenses to Florida and however further they might go.

While the administration may not have been excited about the team's success, some of the parents, including Marc' mother, wanted everyone to know what the team had accomplished and they took it upon themselves to have "1999 Big East Champions" painted on top of the home dugout roof at Hendricken Field.

The team had the better part of a week to savor their victory and prepare for the next round of playoffs in Florida. And enjoy it they did. Bradley Café welcomed the boys, and even Stork got in on the celebration. He had his first drink that week. Rob Corraro himself partook of a Bud Light and a mixed drink later the same night.

Coach Hickey had his own secret concern that the long season and emotional conference playoff victory may have taken its toll on his team. And he may have been right.

CHAPTER 14   NCAA REGIONALS

PUT UP OR SHUT UP

The venue for the next round of the playoffs was unlike anything the Friar players had experienced before, and something for which they had not been prepared, including the media coverage. There were a lot of stories and reports about the plight of their program, playing their last season at Providence College. Everyone seemed to know who they were, including the women in the Tallahassee bars, who paid them more attention than they were used to from the girls at PC. For a few days, they partied like rock stars, especially the relief pitchers and position players who didn't play every day.

For Coach O'Connor, the trip started off, if not a sour note, certainly on a funky one when a bottle of his horse liniment exploded in his luggage and got all over everything inside. The hotel washed all his clothes for him, but they still smelled like shit all week, and you knew when he was near because the smell of that crap got to you a full minute before he did.

Now that everyone knew who the Friars were, they entered the regionals with a reputation of another kind. The umpires were also aware of them, and their dugout demeanor; behavior that would not be tolerated in this round. Before their first game, and prior to the start of every subsequent game, tournament officials warned the team that they had better keep quiet and just play baseball or pay the consequences.

When Marc DesRoches took the ball for the Friars in the opener against Jacksonville, he came out with a lot of confidence, showing good command of his pitches. The game was scoreless until the top of the 3rd, an inning in which Marc started off by striking out the first two hitters before a walk and three consecutive singles yielded a pair of runs. That remained the only scoring until the Friars came up in the bottom of the 5th and pushed three runs of their own across the plate. Neal McCarthy started the inning off with a hit batsman followed by a walk to Angelo. A groundout by Dan Conway moved the runners along and a walk to Jamie Athas loaded the bases for Jason Hairston, who promptly delivered a bases clearing double. The Friars threatened for more, but after a couple more walks they left the bases loaded and clinging to a slim 3-2 lead. That score, however, did not hold up very long. In the top of the 6th, a one out walk and an error opened the door to a four-run inning for the Dolphins. Jacksonville extended their lead to 7-3 with another run in the 8th. But, as it had been with this Friar team all season, they did not give up. Angelo led off the bottom of the 9th with a walk. After Dan Conway singled, Jay Hairston singled with one out knocking in his fourth run of the game. Dan scored on a groundout by Scooter, making it a 7-5 game. With two outs, Coach Hickey went to his bench, sending in Coley O'Donnell to hit for Paul Costello to get the lefty-righty matchup. The Friars big bats were coming up, all of them capable of hitting the ball out of the park and getting them team back into the game. It wasn't meant to be, however, as Coley went down swinging.

Despite the 7-5 opening-round loss to Jacksonville, it did not dampen the spirits of the Friar team. When they came back the next morning, there seemed to be plenty of game left in them.

In the losers bracket, Providence was pitted against the 41-18 Citadel Bulldogs. Neal McCarthy staked lefty starter, Andy Scott, to a three-run lead before he even threw his first pitch when he drilled a three-run bomb in the top of the 1st inning. Stork would give one run back in the bottom half of the inning, but that would be all he would surrender in his eight innings of work. Todd Murray would finish things with a scoreless 9th. In between was a whole lot of Friar offense. The final was 12-1. The big inning for the Friars was the 6th, when they scored six, highlighted by a grand slam off the bat of Angelo Ciminiello.

ONE FOR THE AGES

The defeat eliminated the Bulldogs, who had been crushed 24-6 by Florida State in their opening round tilt. After Florida defeated Jacksonville 9-2, Providence was given a chance to avenge their previous loss to the Dolphins in a 1:00 rematch the next day, May 30, in what would turn out to be one of the most dramatic games of the season.

The Dolphins jumped out to 4-0 lead off Rob Corraro and the Friars in the 1st. Scooter started the home half of the inning with a single. After a one-out walk to Okie, Keith was hit by a pitch to load the bases. Neal McCarthy singled home one run and Providence seemed poised for a big inning of their own. However, Angelo swung at the first-pitch fastball and hit a bullet that was ticked for left field. Unfortunately, it was grabbed by the shortstop, who snared the ball then whirled and fired to first, doubling up Neal who strayed too far off the base.

Jacksonville got the run back in the top of the 2nd inning on a homerun by first baseman, Josh Hurrell. Rob settled down after that, blanking Jacksonville for the next three innings. Opposing pitcher, Palmer Ebanks, shut the Providence offense down, and after five innings the Friars were trailing 5-1. In the top of the 6th, Jacksonville extended their lead, scoring a pair of runs and chasing Rob Corraro from the game. Behind 7-1, Providence's chances of extending their season was not looking very good.

Because the game was played at the home of the Florida State Seminoles, many of their fans turned out to see all the games. They, too, were captivated by the Providence team, aware of what they had gone through that year, the success they had in the wake of the news that their program was going to be cut at the end of the season. One passionate group of Florida fans, known as The Animals, were sitting up in Section B as the Dolphins opened up a six-run lead against the Friars and seemed to be coasting to the championship game against their team, FSU. At this point, the Animals, who had quietly been rooting for Providence, began cheering more vehemently for them. They liked the fire they saw in the team, they way they competed between the lines, as well as outside the lines, in the dugout, chattering constantly, getting on the opposing players and rallying around one another. Providence was fighting for their baseball lives, and as more calls went against PC, both the Friars and the Animals became more vocal. When Jeremy Sweet, who wasn't playing, got tossed from the game by officials for nearly instigating a bench-clearing brawl, it seemed to be just what the Friars needed to get going. It seemed to spark the team, and Providence began to mount a comeback.

The Friars pushed two runs across in the $6^{th,}$ which cut the deficit to 7-3. Providence wasn't done yet. They would continue to chip away. During the 7th inning stretch, the Animals seemed to sense that something was going to happen. They moved en masse behind the Friars dugout along the third base line and sat among the Providence fans, helping them root for a team that appeared to be playing its last game ever. The collective noise from both fan bases was noticed by the Friar players, who responded immediately. That inning, Paul Costello singled with one out, followed a walk to Mike O'Keefe. After Keith Reed flied deep to center, Neal McCarthy delivered a clutch two-out RBI single.

Josh Burnham, who had come into the game to relieve Rob in the 6th, got out of a bases-loaded jam in the 7th and a two-out triple in the 8th without any further damage. When the Friars came to bat in the bottom of the inning, down 7-4, they were six outs away from the end of their season. With time running out, Dan Conway got things started with a single. Jamie Athas followed with a base hit, putting runners on first and second with nobody out. After Jason Hairston moved them up ninety feet with a sacrifice bunt, Scooter walked to load the bases. Jacksonville manager, Terry Alexander, decided to lift his starter after 143 pitches to bring in a fresh arm. Right-hander, Joel Hegeman was brought in to face Paul Costello, and the move paid off for the Dolphins as the Friars' second baseman flew out to right field for the second out. It wasn't deep enough to risk sending Dan home from third, so the bases remained juiced with two outs now for Mike O'Keefe. Jacksonville made another pitching change, calling on Scott Porter, another right-hander out of the bullpen. This time the strategy backfired, and Okie smoked the first pitch into centerfield scoring Dan and Jamie. Keith Reed was up next, and his single brought in Scooter with the game-tying run. The Friars and all their fans, the locals as well as the Providence faithful, were ecstatic. It was a new game, and they had an opportunity to pull out in front. With a chance be the hero, Neal McCarthy walked to load the bases and passed the baton to Angelo. The stadium was buzzing, and when Angelo drove a fastball on a line to right the crowd seemed to hold their breath for a moment. The ball found the glove of the outfielder, who was positioned perfectly and made the final putout of the inning. But the Providence had battered around and scored three times to tie the game at seven.

In the final frame, the Dolphins' James Rodgers, a big 6-foot, 270-lb sophomore was inserted as a pinch-hitter. On the second pitch of the at-bat, he slugged a leadoff homerun that quickly silenced the crowd at Howser Stadium. Just when everything had turned around and seemed to be going the Friars' way, one swing of the bat changed everything. The disappointment in the crowd was palpable, as many thought that Providence was finally done.

Batting in the bottom of the 9th and trailing 8-7, the Friars got a break when Dan Conway opened the inning by reaching base on an error by the Jacksonville second baseman. Jamie Athas was asked to bunt and laid down a beauty, sacrificing Dan to second to get the tying run into scoring position. Jason Hairston was up next and he grounded to third for the second out. Scooter was the team's last chance and the freshman delivered, driving a 3-2 pitch deep to right-center. The ball split the defenders and one-hopped the wall. Dan scored easily, knotting the game at eight as Scooter coasted into third standing up. The gapper brought the stadium to their feet, amazed by the game they were witnessing and cheering appreciatively. After coming all the way back from a 7-1 deficit to tie the game, only to lose the lead in the top of the 9th, Providence had came back a second time. Now Scooter was just ninety feet away representing the winning run, but Paul Costello took a called third strike and the game went into extra innings. Josh Burnham surrendered a two-out double in the 10th but quickly induced a fly out on the next pitch, giving the Friars an opportunity to win in the bottom of the inning.

After two quick outs, Neal McCarthy was at the plate. On a 2-2 offering he struck a hard, low liner that looked to be headed for the centerfield wall, but somehow the ball carried over the fence for a game-winning, walk-off homerun and a stunning 9-8 come-from-behind victory for PC.

The freshman DH threw his arms up in the air and shouted when he saw that the ball cleared the wall. His teammates rushed out onto the field, and as soon as he touched home plate he was buried beneath a pile of swarming Friars. Jeremy Sweet, relegated to sitting in the stands after his ejection, could not be contained. Nothing was going to stop him as he jumped the wall behind the Providence dugout and joined his team jumping up and down on the field, celebrating like Little Leaguers.

The Providence fans were cheering and high-fiving in the stands. The Animals were right there with them, smiling from ear to ear and shaking their heads in disbelief at the same time. Some of the players even seemed stunned by what had just happened. After congratulating the Friar fans, the Animals wished them luck and offered them hearty good-byes and handshakes, even though the next game they would be on opposite sides of the stadium when their respective teams clashed in the regional final later that same day, in fact, in just about an hour from that very moment.

REGIONAL FINALS

At 5:30 p.m., just a short time after that emotional come-from-behind win, the Friars were back on the field against a tough Florida State team. The Seminoles came out and showed everyone why their team was ranked so high. They controlled the game on both sides of the ball, pounding out fifteen hits while a quartet of pitchers allowed only four to Providence.

Sophomore southpaw Mike Stuart started the game and gave it his all, but he and the Friars were simply overmatched that day as Florida State rolled to a 14-3 victory. Stewy took the loss hard, but his teammates had nothing but praise for the effort he gave that afternoon and all season long. Scooter, his roommate, was someone who saw firsthand just how hard he had worked that year. From getting in shape and strengthening his arm to working on the control and command of his pitches, no one busted his hump more than Stewy. A run of bad luck with his arm hampered him all season, but to his credit he kept working and never gave up. He earned a lot of respect from his roommate as well as his teammates. The way Florida had been playing during the tournament, no one could have stopped them.

One touching and unexpected moment came after it became imminently apparent that the Friars did not have another comeback left in them. The Florida State fans once again showed a lot of class and demonstrated an appreciation for the plight of the Providence team. In the 9th inning the Animals joined the Providence fans in saluting the team with a rousing standing ovation that lasted pretty much the duration the inning. They were clapping and chanting, "Friars! Friars!" the whole time.

After the inevitable final out was made, the cheering continued. Even the Florida State players gathered in the infield and applauded. An announcement was made acknowledging the Friar players and coaches. "Thanks for the Memories, Providence Friars" flashed across the scoreboard. It would have been difficult for anyone not to experience a deep emotional response to what they were witnessing. There may not have been a completely dry eye in the stadium.

The Friar players consoled and congratulated one another on a remarkable season. As they made their way out of the stadium, many of the Animals joined the Providence fans and formed a line from the field gate to the stadium exit, shaking hands and applauding each player and coach as they walked out. The Friars and their fans were invited by the Animals to attend a tailgate party over in one of the lots for beer and BBQ. The FSU fans hoped they would be taken up on their offer, but did not figure the Friars would show up. Ten minutes later, however, the Animals looked towards Howser Stadium and saw the entire Providence baseball team and their supporters headed their way.

What followed was one big party, a celebration for FSU moving on in the playoffs as well as a tribute to the Providence College Friars final season of baseball. It was something that their own school would not afford them, so when the Florida fans extended the invitation there was no way the Friars could refuse. The tears that had been shed earlier had been replaced by laughter as the players and the fans shared stories, drank and ate. Friendships were made that day that have lasted more than ten years now. In parting, both sides wished each other well. Handshakes and waves were replaced by hugs and kisses. When the Providence bus pulled out of the parking lot, a lot of the Friars were wearing Animal T-shirts and carrying Animal Songbooks while the Animals were wearing Providence hats, shirts and even game jerseys.

CHAPTER 15   THROWING IN THE COWL

THE MUSIC STOPS

A lot of people had been holding out hope, even at the very end, that the baseball program would be saved, especially after the season the team had and all the support they were shown by everyone except the school administration. There were those who believed that some rescuer would arrive at the eleventh hour to grant PC baseball a reprieve. Several attempts had been made by local businesses, some owned by alumni, who offered to donate money to keep the baseball program going. The pledges reached into the millions of dollars, but the program could not be bought. The college informed everyone who wanted to donate money that they were free to do so, but that the institution would be obligated to disburse the money equally among all PC athletic programs, not just baseball.

It seemed as if the powers that be at Providence had written the sport off long ago, so there would be no knight in shining armor that would come to save baseball at Providence College. When the team got back home and arrived on campus, there was no one there to receive them, let alone organize a cookout or a ticker-tape parade. School was out for the summer, and with the offices cleaned out and everything packed up it was as if they were ghosts. At that moment, at least, the only thing they had to prove that they ever really existed were the momentos they collected, including each other's jerseys that they signed and exchanged.

That was it. The music had stopped. The season was over for the 1999 Friars, and for baseball at Providence College. While that reality was still settling in, there was time to reflect on the season and the place that the 1999 team and the players would have in the school's all-time record book.

GAUDY STATISTICS

Baseball has always been a game of statistics, and there are plenty of them to support just how good the 1999 Friar baseball team was, but at the same time they do not show the heart and pride that this team played with all season.

To begin with, their 47 wins was a new school record, surpassing the mark of 44 set in 1995, the only other year that a Friar team won more than forty games in a season. Their fifteen game winning streak established a new record that would last forever. Their total of 18 Big East wins against only 8 defeats also became a Providence College best. This, after beginning the season 1-5 in Big East play.

Contributions for the team's success came from all the players.

Providence had already swept the Big East postseason Awards, but there were more honors to bestow upon the 1999 squad.

PC players also dominated the All-New England Division I team, with eight members selected along with skipper Charlie Hickey, who was chosen as the New England Coach Of The Year. First Team honors included Marc DesRoches, Angelo Ciminiello, Mike Scott and Keith Reed. Josh Burnham, Dan Conway, Mike O'Keefe and Neal McCarthy were Second Team selections.

Marc DesRoches, Keith Reed and Mike Scott were also named to the All-Big East first team, Angelo Ciminiello to the second team.

Joining Mike "Scooter" Scott on the All-Rookie team was Jamie Athas and Neal McCarthy, a trio of talented, young players who played a big part in the team's championship season.

Scooter's .428 overall batting average was second all-time at PC, surpassed only by Don Mezzanotte's .477 in 1960. His average never dipped below .400 all season. His 175 total bases would place him second all-time at PC behind only his teammate, Keith Reed, who had 179 that same year. He also established a new school record with 269 at-bats. Scooter and Neal shared the team lead in doubles (21). Neal added fifteen homeruns, a Providence College rookie record.

Jamie Athas contributed everywhere, especially on the base paths, swiping eighteen bases in twenty-one attempts to lead the team. The freshman shortstop played in 60 games and made just 2 errors in his last 19 games, while participating in 42 of the team's 62 twin killings.

Keith Reed was named the Eastern Collegiate Conference Player Of The Year for his outstanding season, which included a PC record 74-RBI. He became the first and only ballplayer in Providence College history to win the award. That summer, Keith was drafted in the first round, 23rd pick overall, by the Baltimore Orioles.

With an offense that produced 10 or more runs twenty-three times and 20 of more runs five times in 1999, the Friars bats were a major factor in the team's overall success. Their consistency at the plate was evidenced in their .342 Big East batting average and .341 overall BA, the best ever in the history of the program. The team's 86 homeruns established a single-season high, eclipsing by six the total the Friars hit the previous season. The Friars also set new team records for runs (576), hits (745), doubles (146), triples (29), homeruns (86) total bases (1,207) and RBI (510).

Pitching contributions came from both expected and unexpected sources. Marc DesRoches' 14 victories and 82 strike outs in 1999 would be forever listed as tops in PC history, but he gave so much more as a leader on a team with so many young players. Josh Burnham finished the season with a new Friar record, throwing 107 innings. He proved to be a workhorse for the team all season long. Of his fifteen appearances, eight of those were complete games. With Rob Corraro's 8-2 mark, the three starters combined to win 31 games against only seven defeats.

The PC pitching corps chipped in to save 10 victories, the most since the 1991 club saved eleven, and just two shy of the all-time school record of twelve. Stork led the Friars that year with four saves. The southpaw also won six games as a starter and boasted a highly respectable 4.02 ERA.

Defensively, the 62 double plays the Friars turned were tops in the conference and just short of the PC record of 65 set in 1996. Mike O'Keefe may have been the most consistent glove man for the Friars, having been involved in 44 of the team's 62 double plays turned that season. Working the first base bag as well as some outfield, Okie had a fielding percentage of .982, committing only 8 errors in 450 chances. He was also consistent at the plate, batting .349 with 17 doubles, 12 homers and 68 RBI. Only five other players in PC baseball history drove in more than 60 runs in a season, three of which were his teammates that year. Okie played in all 61 games that season, as did Keith Reed.

PAST, PRESENT, FUTURE

In 80 baseball seasons at Providence College, the teams combined for a record of 1,131 – 856 – 13, a .569 winning percentage. The best may have been yet to come, but we'll never know. The success of the 1999 season, together with what the baseball program had been doing throughout the 90's, certainly would have continued to attract the best high school ballplayers from around the region to PC. The talented freshman and sophomores that would have been returning for the 2000 season with Big East experience would have made the Friars strong contenders to repeat as conference champions and maybe advance further in the NCAA's. Only nine of the players were graduating or in their last year of eligibility in 1999, but the next fall all of them would be somewhere else, scattered around the country, some playing baseball, some not. But no matter where they ended up in 2000 and beyond, they would always have the magic and the memories they shared during the 1999 season at Providence College.

1999 Providence College Friars

Name	Pos.	Year	Ht.	Wt.	T/B	AV	HR	RBI
Mike Scott	LF	So.	5-10	160	L	.428	5	61
Paul Costello	2B	Sr.	6-2	185	R	.325	2	42
Mike O'Keefe	1B	So.	5-11	205	L	.349	12	68
Keith Reed	RF	Jr.	6-4	215	R	.405	17	74
Neal McCarthy	DH	Fr.	5-11	165	R/L	.374	15	62
Angelo Ciminiello	3B	Sr.	6-1	195	R	.339	13	54
Dan Conway	C	So.	6-0	185	R	.327	10	49
Jaime Athas	SS	Fr.	6-1	180	R/L	.316	5	42
Jason Hairston	CF	Jr.	5-8	165	R	.247	0	6
Matt Ciardelli	2B/ss	Fr.	6-0	185	R	.111	0	1
Coley O'Donnell	1B/DH	Jr.	6-2	220	L	.278	2	22
Jeremy Sweet	DH/1B	Jr.	6-2	205	R	.235	4	20
Brendan Trainor	2B/3B	Fr.	6-0	180	R/L	.233	1	9
Chris Caprio	C	Sr.	5-11	205	R	.000	0	0
Brendan Ryan	OF/P	Fr.	6-3	190	R	.000	0	0

Name		Year	Ht.	Wt.	W	L	IP	ERA	K	BB
Marc DesRoches	RHP	Gr.	6-2	220	14	1	96.2	2.70	82	23
Josh Burnham	RHP	Sr.	5-11	170	9	3	107	5.55	68	35
Rob Corraro	RHP	Sr.	6-7	215	8	3	98.2	5.20	41	34
Andy Scott	LHP	So.	6-1	165	6	2	65	4.02	40	31
Brett Donovan	LHP	So.	6-0	160	1	0	13.2	1.98	11	4
Scott Swanjord	RHP	Sr.	6-5	225	0	0	13.1	3.38	6	6
Ryan Lewis	LHP	Fr.	5-11	205	6	2	52	6.06	43	17
Mike Stuart	LHP	So.	5-10	175	2	2	27	9.22	23	10
Todd Murray	RHP	Sr.	6-1	180	0	1	17.1	9.87	13	13
Josh Cox	RHP	Sr.	5-11	175	1	0	13	11.77	2	0

Former Providence College Players
Drafted by Major League Baseball Teams

Ed Wineapple	1929	Washington Senators
Phil Welch	1975	Boston Red Sox
Roger Haggerty	1986	Boston Red Sox
Jim Navilliat	1986	Oakland A's
Ed Walsh	1987	Chicago White Sox
Mark Loughlin	1991	Houston Astros
Mike Kendzierski	1992	Toronto Blue Jays (H.S.)
Lou Merloni	1993	Boston Red Sox
Jim Foster	1993	Baltimore Orioles
Bob O'Toole	1995	Baltimore Orioles
Rob Corraro	1995	Toronto Blue Jays (H.S.)
Pete Tucci	1996	Toronto Blue Jays
John McDonald	1996	Cleveland Indians
Todd Incantalupo	1997	Milwaukee Brewers
Mike O'Keefe	1999	Anaheim Angels
Keith Reed	1999	Baltimore Orioles
Dan Conway	2000	Colorado Rockies (Wake Forest)
Jamie Athas	2001	S.F. Giants (Wake Forest)
Mike Scott	2001	Detroit Tigers (UCONN)

WHERE ARE THEY NOW

Jamie Athas went on to Wake Forest University, where he was drafted as a junior and signed with the San Francisco Giants. He played six years, getting up to AAA. Jamie left pro ball in 2006 and is currently working as an Assistant Coach at UNC, Greensboro.

Chris Caprio graduated from Providence in 1999, then went on to get his Masters Degree in Accounting from Bentley University. Chris currently works as the North American Corporate Controller for Altran USA, a financial and engineering consulting firm in Boston. He resides in Medford, MA with his wife, Meghan, and two daughters, Melissa and Rori.

Angelo Ciminiello married his girlfriend from PC. They now live in CT with their two young sons and are awaiting the birth of their third child as of this writing. After leaving Providence in 1999, Angelo attended medical school in Philadelphia. Upon graduation from Jefferson Medical College in 2003, he began his residency in orthopedic surgery at the University of Connecticut Health Center in Farmington. In 2008 he began a year-long Sports Medicine Fellowship at New England Baptist Hospital in Boston and is now in practice in Danbury, CT with Danbury Orthopedic Associates.

George Colli graduated from PC in 2001 and returned home, first becoming the Assistant Director of Admissions at Suffield Academy in CT, the high school from which he graduated, and in 2003 working as a real estate broker in the family business. In 2008, George was the Democratic nominee to the CT State Senate out of the 7th District. George currently resides in New York City and is pursuing a career in Journalism.

Dan Conway went to Wake Forest, where he played alongside, and was a roommate of Jamie Athas. Dan was selected in the 8th round of the 2000 amateur entry draft by the Colorado Rockies. He played in the Minor Leagues until 2007, getting as high as AAA.

Paul Costello married his college girlfriend and is working as an account manager for a pharmaceutical company out of Massachusetts, where he and his wife live.

Josh Cox graduated from PC and returned home to Cambridge, MA. He quickly secured a job in Boston at the Federal Reserve Bank doing Information Systems and later IT work, during which time he completed his MBA at Bentley University. He married his wife Donna in 2007, and the couple soon moved to New York when Josh took a position with *Scholastic*, in Manhattan.

Marc DesRoches is single and lives in Cambridge, MA. He works for the *RBI Baseball Academy* in Foxboro.

Mike O'Keefe was drafted in the 12th round of the 1999 draft by the Anaheim Angels. He played 6 years of pro ball, getting as high as AAA. Mike is married and runs *Mike O'Keefe's Baseball Academy* in New Haven, CT.

Keith Reed was drafted in the first round of the 1999 draft by the Baltimore Orioles. He worked his way up through the minor leagues and made his Major League debut in 2005, when he was called up to take Sammy Sosa's place on the O's roster at the end of the season. Keith joined the Newark Bears of the independent Atlantic League in 2007.

Andy Scott went on to play ball at Belmont Abbey College outside Charlotte, VA, where he graduated in 2002. In 2007, he received his M Ed from Christian Brothers. Stork stayed in baseball as a coach, currently at Rhodes College in Memphis, TN, where he lives with his wife, Laura.

Mike Scott transferred to the University of Connecticut after the 1999 season at PC. In 2001 he hit .413, breaking the UCONN single-season hits record and was named the Big East Player of the Year. Scooter was taken in the 23rd round of the MLB Draft by the Detroit Tigers, spending two seasons in the minors before an elbow injury ended his playing career. Scooter currently resides in Trumbull, CT with my wife Catherine. He is a math teacher and the head varsity baseball coach at his alma mater, Darien High School.

Mike Stuart went to Boston College to finish his baseball and academic career. He later married a girl he went to high school with and he and his wife, Andrea, reside in their hometown of Canton, MA. Stewy works for an in-house advertising agency for a large investment company in Boston. He no longer plays baseball, but he competes in a competitive softball league.

Scott Swanjord received his law degree from Widener University School of Law in 2002. Swanny is now an attorney specializing in Rule Of Law and Federal Government contracting in the Washington D.C./Richmond area, where he lives with his wife, Kathy, who is also an attorney.

Jeremy Sweet lives in Fall River, MA with his beautiful wife Krystal working for Comcast as a Direct Sales Rep.

Charlie Hickey went on and became the head baseball coach for Central Connecticut State University, where he has been for the last ten years since leaving Providence. Under his guidance, the Blue Devils have won three of the last eight Northeast Conference Championships, advancing to the NCAA Tournament in each of those seasons. Coach Hickey was named the NEC Coach of the Year for the third time in 2006.

John Rinaldo left PC as an athletic strength coach in 2002, and has since traveled down a new career path. John is now a writer/producer/director for WHI$KY MONEY PRODUCTIONS in Worcester, MA. He made a short film, "The Casket," which received admittance to the Aisle 5 Film Festival in Boston in 2005. John has also studied acting, landing supporting roles in a few short films and an independent feature.

John Rock is the current Assistant Director of Sports Medicine at Providence College. He was not with the 1999 team during the regular season but re-joined the Friars for the Big East and NCAA playoffs. He lives in Cranston with his wife Patty and three children, Patrick, Abby and Maggie.

Joe Valenzano graduated from PC in 2000. He went on to earn his Master's Degree from the University of Maine, where he also worked as a volunteer baseball coach, assisting the Black Bears head coach and former PC skipper, Paul Kostacopoulous. Joe then moved on to Georgia State University, serving as an administrative assistant for the baseball team while he worked on his PhD in Public Communication. In 2006, he took a teaching position at the University of Nevada, Las Vegas.